Highlights

Highlights of GAO-12-73, a report to congressional requesters

ARIZONA BORDER REGION

Federal Agencies Could Better Utilize Law Enforcement Resources in Support of Wildland Fire Management Activities

Why GAO Did This Study

Wildland fires can result from both natural and human causes. Human-caused wildland fires are of particular concern in Arizona—especially within 100 miles of the U.S.-Mexico border because this is a primary area of entry for illegal border crossers and GAO has previously reported that illegal border crossers have been suspected of igniting wildland fires. Over half of the land in the Arizona border region is managed by the federal government—primarily by the Department of Agriculture's Forest Service and four agencies within the Department of the Interior. These agencies collaborate with state, tribal, and local entities to respond to wildland fires. GAO was asked to examine, for the region, the (1) number, cause, size, and location of wildland fires from 2006 through 2010; (2) economic and environmental effects of human-caused wildland fires burning 10 or more acres; (3) extent to which illegal border crossers were the ignition source of wildland fires on federal lands; and (4) ways in which the presence of illegal border crossers has affected fire suppression activities. GAO reviewed interagency policies and procedures; analyzed wildland fire data; and interviewed federal, tribal, state, and local officials, as well as private citizens.

What GAO Recommends

GAO recommends, among other things, that the agencies develop strategies for selecting fires to investigate and establish a risk-based approach for utilizing law enforcement resources. In their comments on a draft of this report, the Forest Service and the Department of the Interior generally agreed with these recommendations.

View GAO-12-73 or key components. For more information, contact Anu K. Mittal at (202) 512-3841 or mittala@gao.gov.

What GAO Found

From 2006 through 2010, at least 2,467 wildland fires occurred in the Arizona border region. Of this number, 2,126, or about 86 percent, were caused by human activity. The majority of these fires—1,364—burned less than 1 acre each. About 63 percent or 1,553 of the 2,467 fires were ignited on federally managed land or tribal land.

Human-caused wildland fires that burned 10 or more acres had a number of economic and environmental impacts on the Arizona border region, but these impacts cannot be fully quantified because comprehensive data are not available. Specifically, these fires resulted in (1) over $35 million in fire suppression costs by federal and state agencies, (2) destruction of property, (3) impacts on ranching operations, and (4) impacts on tourism. Similarly, these fires had several environmental impacts, such as the expansion of nonnative plant species, degraded endangered species habitat, and soil erosion. However, the full economic and environmental impacts cannot be determined because complete information about these impacts is not available.

The total number of fires ignited by illegal border crossers on federal lands in the Arizona border region is not fully known, in part because federal land management agencies have not conducted investigations of all human-caused wildland fires that occurred on these lands, as called for by agency policy, and the agencies do not have a strategy for selecting fires they do investigate. Of the 422 human-caused wildland fires that occurred on Forest Service, Interior, or tribal lands and burned at least 1 acre from 2006 through 2010, only 77 were investigated. According to land management agency officials, the lack of trained fire investigators was the primary reason for the limited number of investigations. Of the investigations conducted, 30 identified illegal border crossers as a suspected source of ignition. Agency policy notes that identifying trends in fire causes is critical to the success of fire prevention programs, but without better data on the specific ignition sources of human-caused wildland fires in the region, the agencies are hampered in their ability to target their efforts to prevent future wildland fires.

The presence of illegal border crossers has complicated fire suppression activities in the Arizona border region. According to agency officials, the presence of illegal border crossers has increased concerns about firefighter safety and, in some instances, has required firefighters to change or limit the tactics they use in suppressing fires. For example, the presence of illegal border crossers has limited firefighting activities at night and complicated the use of aerial firefighting methods. The agencies have taken some steps to mitigate the risks to firefighters by, for example, using law enforcement to provide security. However, none of the agencies have developed or implemented a risk-based approach for addressing these challenges. Consequently, law enforcement resources are routinely dispatched to all fires regardless of the risk, which may prevent the agencies from using their limited resources most efficiently. Moreover, while the Forest Service has developed a formal policy for addressing the risks to firefighters in the region, the other agencies have neither formally adopted this policy nor developed their own.

_____ **United States Government Accountability Office**

Contents

Tables

Figures

November 8, 2011

Congressional Requesters

A natural part of many ecosystems, wildland fires can have devastating effects on communities, damage sensitive ecosystems, and be costly to suppress. Wildland fires may be ignited by lightning or as a result of human activities, such as improperly extinguished campfires, sparks from equipment and vehicles, or recreational shooting. Fires triggered by natural causes are inevitable and play an important ecological role on many landscapes, but human-caused wildland fires can damage areas that might not otherwise experience fire or that might burn with less frequency or severity.[1] The recent Horseshoe Two and Monument fires in southern Arizona provide vivid examples of the devastation that can result from human-caused wildland fires. The Horseshoe Two Fire burned nearly 223,000 acres in May and June 2011, mostly on the Coronado National Forest, and cost millions to suppress. Similarly, according to preliminary estimates from the agencies, the Monument Fire burned more than 30,000 acres in the Huachuca Mountains in June and July 2011, destroyed more than 60 homes, and forced thousands of residents living near Sierra Vista, Arizona, to evacuate.[2]

Human-caused wildland fires are of particular concern in Arizona along the Mexico border because southeast Arizona is a primary entry point for illegal border crossers on the U.S. southwestern border. As we reported in December 2010, illegal border crossers have been suspected of starting wildland fires either by accident—for example, from cooking fires that escape—or on purpose—for example, to divert law enforcement resources away from a particular area.[3] In this context, you asked us to examine

---

[1]To achieve land management objectives federal land mangers sometimes use prescribed burns—fires set deliberately by land managers under weather, fuel, and temperature conditions that enable the fire to be controlled at a relatively low intensity level. In this report, we use the term "human-caused wildland fires" to refer only to human-caused fires other than prescr bed burns.

[2]Suppression cost obligations and damages incurred as a result of these fires are estimates reported by federal agencies. We did not independently verify the accuracy of these data.

[3]GAO, *Federal Lands: Adopting a Formal, Risk-Based Approach Could Help Land Management Agencies Better Manage Their Law Enforcement Resources*, GAO-11-144 (Washington, D.C.: Dec. 17, 2010).

wildland fires that occurred in Arizona within 100 miles of the U.S.-Mexico border during the previous 5 years.[4] For such wildland fires, this report examines (1) their number, cause, size, and location; (2) the economic and environmental effects of human-caused wildland fires that burned 10 or more acres; (3) the extent to which federal agencies determined that illegal border crossers were the ignition source of wildland fires on federal and tribal lands; and (4) ways in which the presence of illegal border crossers has affected fire suppression activities in this area.

To determine the extent of wildland fire occurrence in the Arizona border region, we collected federal and state wildland fire occurrence data from databases at the National Interagency Fire Center (NIFC)[5] for fires that occurred within Arizona during calendar years 2006 through 2010.[6] From these data, we identified those wildland fires that occurred within 100 miles of the Arizona-Mexico border. For these fires, we then analyzed the data to identify the acreage burned and general cause—human or natural—cited for ignition. We assessed the reliability of the data we used by reviewing information about the underlying database systems and discussing the data with agency officials responsible for managing these databases, and determined that the data were sufficiently reliable for the purposes of presenting acreage burned and general cause of wildland fires. We also obtained information from the Department of Defense regarding wildland fire incidents on its lands in the region—which is not included in NIFC's data—and included these data in our overall analysis. We identified those human-caused wildland fires that burned 10 or more acres (referred to as significant fires for the purposes of this report) and

---

[4]In this report we refer to the area in Arizona that is within 100 miles of the U.S.-Mexico border as the Arizona border region.

[5]NIFC, located in Boise, ID, is the nation's logistical support center for controlling and extinguishing wildland fires and coordinates the mobilization of fire suppression supplies, equipment, and personnel at the federal, regional, and local levels. Additionally, NIFC maintains historical fire occurrence data for the Department of Agriculture's Forest Service and the Department of the Interior's Bureau of Indian Affairs, Bureau of Land Management, Fish and Wildlife Service, and National Park Service. NIFC also maintains historical fire occurrence data collected by state agencies, including the Arizona State Forestry Division, for fires on nonfederal lands.

[6]Unless otherwise noted, all references in this report are to calendar years rather than fiscal years. We did not include fires that occurred in calendar year 2011 because federal agencies do not collect fire documentation from local units or conduct quality assurance checks on data until the end of the calendar year, and therefore 2011 data were not complete and may not be reliable.

obtained data on suppression cost obligations for those fires as well as available documentation of economic and environmental effects. In addition, we visited the region and discussed with federal and nonfederal fire suppression and law enforcement officials, as well as private industry representatives and private citizens in the ranching community, their experiences with wildland fire occurrence and suppression activities, as well as the economic and environmental damage as a result of human-caused wildland fires. To assess the extent to which federal agencies determined that illegal border crossers were the ignition source of these fires, we reviewed agency documents to identify criteria for conducting investigations into the ignition source of human-caused wildland fires. We also collected and analyzed fire investigation reports to evaluate the extent to which fire investigations were conducted for human-caused wildland fires that burned 1 or more acres and, for those fires for which investigations were conducted, the extent to which officials identified illegal border crossers as the source of ignition. Additionally, we reviewed fire incident reports created by fire response personnel to identify the extent to which they cited illegal border crossers as a potential source of ignition. To determine the ways in which the presence of illegal border crossers has affected fire suppression in the Arizona border region, we reviewed national and regional land management wildland fire guidance to identify any practices unique to regional land management units developed in response to illegal cross-border activity. During our site visits, we also discussed with federal and nonfederal officials their experiences fighting wildland fires in the region.

We conducted this performance audit from December 2010 to November 2011 in accordance with generally accepted government auditing standards. Those standards require that we plan and perform the audit to obtain sufficient, appropriate evidence to provide a reasonable basis for our findings and conclusions based on our audit objectives. We believe that the evidence obtained provides a reasonable basis for our findings and conclusions based on our audit objectives.

Background

The Arizona-Mexico border extends about 370 miles, accounting for almost 20 percent of the 2,000-mile U.S.-Mexico border. About 51 percent of the land in the Arizona border region is managed by the federal government, primarily by the Forest Service within the Department of Agriculture, four agencies within the Department of the Interior—the Bureau of Indian Affairs (BIA), Bureau of Land Management (BLM), Fish and Wildlife Service (FWS), and National Park Service (NPS)—and the Department of Defense (DOD).[7] The remainder of the land is local or private (21 percent), state-managed (16 percent), or tribal (12 percent). Figure 1 shows the areas managed by these various entities.

---

[7]The Department of the Interior's Bureau of Reclamation manages a very small amount of federal land in the Arizona border region. We did not include this agency in our review.

Figure 1: Land Management in the Arizona Border Region

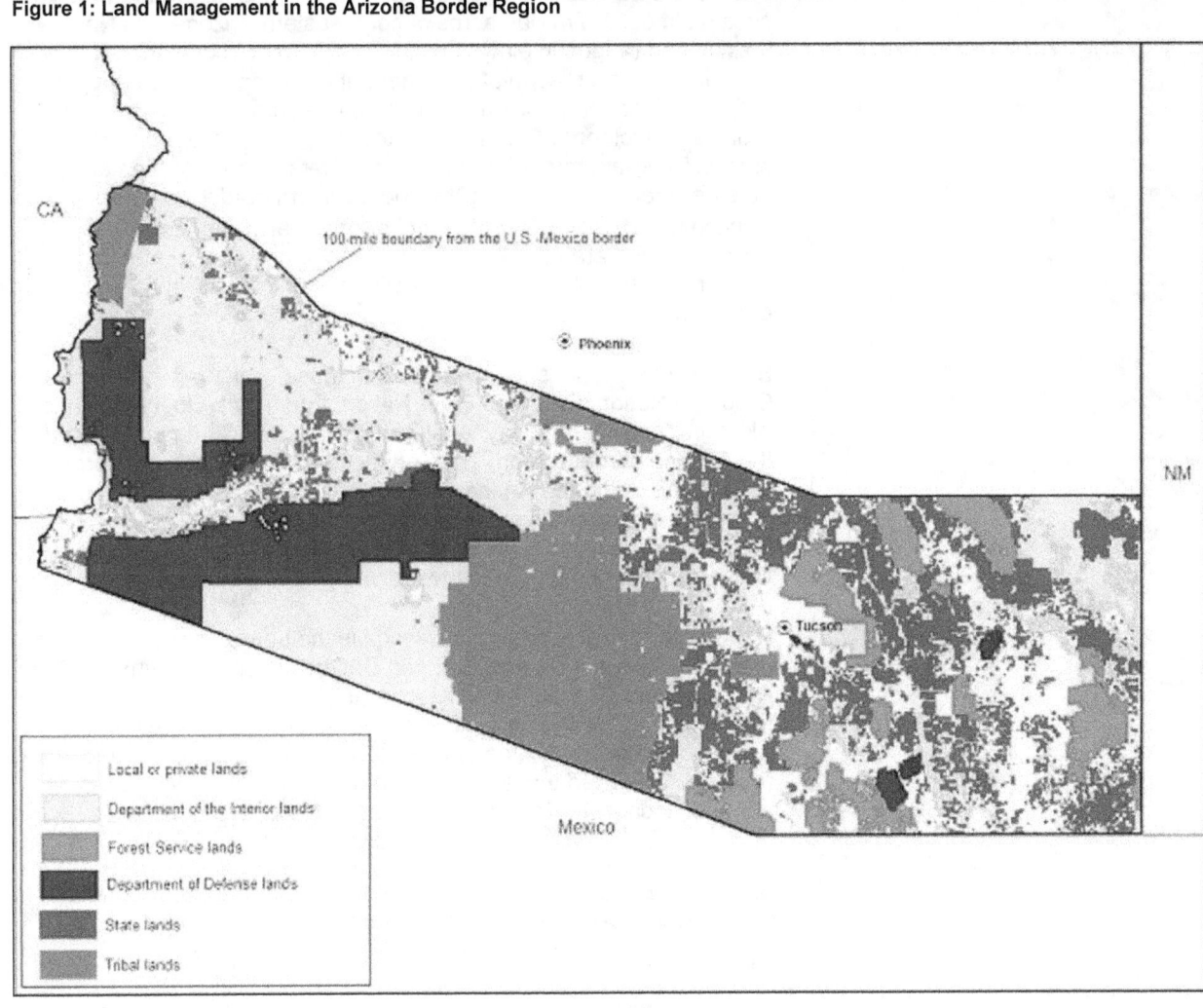

Source: Department of the Interior; Mapinfo (map).

Each federal agency that manages land within the border region has a distinct mission and set of responsibilities, which may include managing the land for multiple uses, such as recreation; conserving natural and historic resources; conserving and enhancing fish, wildlife, plants, and their habitats; and providing rangeland for grazing. Federal agency responsibilities for land units in the Arizona border region include the following:

- The Forest Service manages the Coronado National Forest, which covers almost 1.8 million acres of southeastern Arizona and New Mexico and ranges in elevations from 3,000 feet to over 10,000 feet. In addition to the preservation of natural resources, the forest is used for recreational purposes and ranchers use some of the forest for grazing. In October 2010, we reported that more illegal border crossers migrate through the Coronado National Forest than any other federal land unit along the southwestern border.[8] The Forest Service has reported that the number of illegal border crossers traveling in the area threatens natural resources and creates a dangerous environment for the public and for Forest Service employees.[9]

- BIA provides services to several Indian tribes, including the Tohono O'odham Nation, Colorado River Nation, Fort Yuma-Quechan Nation, Ak-Chin Tribal Community, and Gila River Indian Community within the Arizona border region. The Tohono O'odham Nation, the largest Indian tribe within the Arizona border region, covers about 2.9 million acres, an area approximately the size of Connecticut. Tohono O'odham officials have previously reported that illegal border crossers cause significant damage to their lands.[10]

- BLM manages numerous public lands in the border region, including the nearly half-million-acre Sonoran Desert National Monument, San Pedro National Conservation Area, and Ironwood Forest National Monument. BLM lands are used for multiple purposes, including recreation, grazing, mining, and wildlife habitat. In our November 2010 report, we reported that BLM officials posted warning signs at 11 entrance locations of the Sonoran Desert National Monument to warn

[8]GAO, *Southwest Border: More Timely Border Patrol Access and Training Could Improve Security Operations and Natural Resource Protection on Federal Lands*, GAO-11-38 (Washington, D.C.: Oct. 19, 2010).

[9]*Effects of Illegal Border Activities on the Federal Land Management Agencies, Before the Subcommittee on Interior, Environment, and Related Agencies, House Committee on Appropriations*, 109th Cong. (2006) (statement of Tina J. Terrell, Forest Supervisor, Cleveland National Forest, United States Department of Agriculture).

[10]*Walls and Waivers: Expedited Construction of the Southern Border Wall and Collateral Impacts to Communities and the Environment, Before the Subcommittee on Fisheries, Wildlife, and Oceans and Subcommittee on National Parks, Forests, and Public Lands of the House Committee on Natural Resources*, 110th Cong. (2008) (statement of the Honorable Ned Norris, Jr., Chairman Tohono O'odham Nation).

GAO-12-73 Wildland Fire in the Arizona Border Region

the public against travel on portions of the monument because of potential encounters with illegal border crossers.[11]

- FWS works to preserve and enhance fish, wildlife, plants, and their habitats in wildlife refuges in the region, including the Buenos Aires, Cabeza Prieta, Imperial, and Kofa National Wildlife Refuges. In December 2010, we reported that the Refuge Manager of Buenos Aires National Wildlife Refuge testified before Congress that illegal border crossers have disturbed wildlife and created more than 1,300 miles of illegal trails, causing the loss of vegetation and severe erosion.[12] In addition, a portion of the refuge adjacent to the border has been closed to the public due to safety concerns caused by illegal border crossers.

- NPS is responsible for conserving the scenery, natural and historical objects, and wildlife of the national park system, which includes Coronado National Memorial, Organ Pipe Cactus National Monument, and Saguaro National Park in the Arizona border region. As was the case with the Buenos Aires National Wildlife Refuge, the Organ Pipe Cactus National Monument has previously been closed to the public because of the safety concerns associated with illegal border crossers. Officials at other sites, such as the Fort Bowie National Historic Site, have reported that the cultural and historical integrity of the site has been compromised by illegal border crossers because of the waste they have left in the area—including clothing, cans, water jugs, plastic bags, and human waste.

- DOD manages a number of installations and facilities used for testing and training its forces in the region, including Fort Huachuca, the Yuma Proving Grounds, the Barry M. Goldwater Range, and Davis-Monthan Air Force Base. DOD officials told us that training missions at the Barry M. Goldwater Range have been delayed or altered due to the presence of illegal border crossers.

Additionally, agents of the U.S. Border Patrol—an office within the Department of Homeland Security (DHS)—patrol federal and nonfederal

---

[11]GAO, *Border Security: Additional Actions Needed to Better Ensure a Coordinated Federal Response to Illegal Activity on Federal Lands*, GAO-11-177 (Washington, D.C.: Nov. 18, 2010).

[12]GAO-11-144.

lands near the border to find and apprehend persons who have illegally crossed the U.S. border. Border Patrol is responsible for controlling and guarding the boundaries and borders of the United States against the illegal entry of people who are not citizens or nationals.[13] Border patrol agents have the authority to search, interrogate, and arrest undocumented aliens and others who are engaging in illegal activities, such as illegal entry and smuggling of people, drugs, or other contraband on federal lands and other areas up to 100 miles from the border.

Each of the federal land management agencies also has responsibility to respond to wildland fires on federal lands, while the Arizona State Forestry Division and other entities—including tribal and local fire departments—have primary responsibility for responding to wildland fires on state, local, and private lands. When a wildland fire starts on federal land, federal policy directs federal agencies to consider land management objectives—identified by land and fire management plans developed by each land management unit—and the structures and resources at risk when determining whether and how to suppress it. Historically, the Forest Service and the Interior agencies attempted to suppress all wildland fires quickly because of their potentially damaging effects on local economies and natural environments; in recent decades, however, the agencies fundamentally reassessed their understanding of naturally occurring wildland fire's role on the landscape, and they began to see more benefits from these wildland fires. For instance, fire can limit the spread of insects and diseases, reduce brush and weeds, and return the nutrients to the soil, where they help produce a new generation of plants. For ranchers whose cattle are dependent on the new generation of plants, fire can burn unwanted brush and allow grasses to flourish in future years. If agencies determine that a naturally ignited wildland fire can promote land management objectives, they may use less aggressive fire suppression strategies that not only can reduce fire suppression costs in some cases but can also be safer for firefighters by reducing their exposure to unnecessary risks. In contrast, interagency policy calls for these agencies to initiate suppression activities immediately for all human-caused wildland fires.

Fire suppression efforts are mobilized through an interagency incident management system, which depends on the close cooperation and

---

[13]8 U.S.C. §§ 1101-1537.

coordination of federal, state, tribal, and local fire protection entities. Fighting wildland fires—which can burn across federal, state, and local jurisdictions—can require investments of personnel, aircraft, equipment, and supplies and can result in substantial fire suppression expenditures.

To document fire occurrence, fire personnel prepare a fire incident report, and the information from these reports populates the agencies' fire data management systems. The information collected in these reports includes basic data such as date the fire started, location, general cause (natural or human), number of acres burned, and the date the fire was extinguished. Firefighters can also include narrative information in these reports, such as information about suppression activities or fire cause.

Number, Cause, Size, and Location of Wildland Fires in the Arizona Border Region

From 2006 through 2010, at least 2,467 wildland fires occurred in the Arizona border region. Most of these fires were caused by human activity, burned less than 1 acre each, and were ignited on federal or tribal land. Federal and state agencies determined that 2,126 of these fires, or about 86 percent, were caused by human activities (see fig. 2). This percentage is consistent with the national average for wildland fires caused by human activities; according to NIFC data, about 87 percent of all wildland fires that occurred nationally from 2006 through 2010 were caused by human activities.

Figure 2: Wildland Fires in the Arizona Border Region, by Cause, 2006-2010

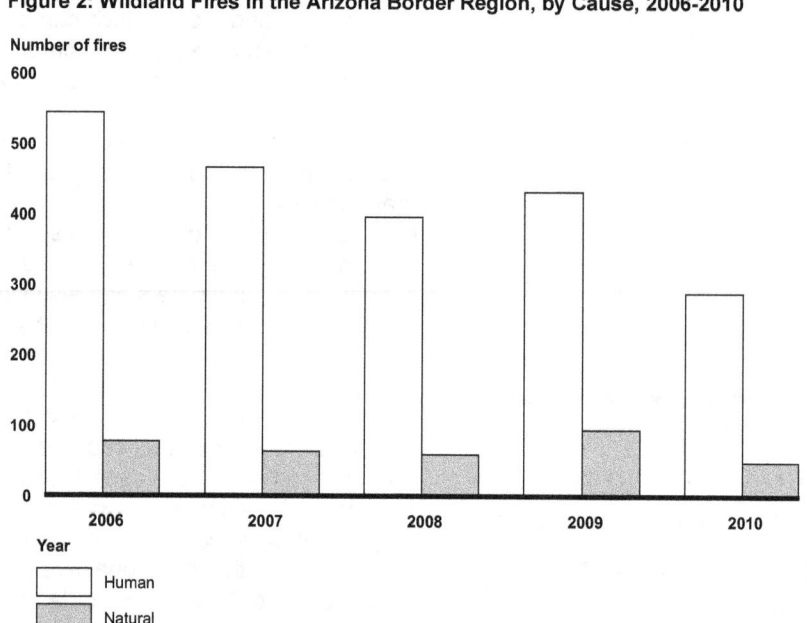

Source: GAO analysis of USDA, Interior, DOD, and Arizona Forestry Division data.

Most of the human-caused wildland fires—1,364, or 64 percent—burned less than 1 acre of land each; 508 fires burned from 1 to 10 acres each; and 241 fires were significant, burning 10 or more acres each.[14] These 241 significant human-caused wildland fires burned a total of more than 123,000 acres, which accounts for about 99 percent of all acres burned during this time by human-caused wildland fire in the region; the largest of these wildland fires—the 2009 Elkhorn Fire—burned more than 23,000 acres. See figure 3 for the location of significant human-caused wildland fires during this period. The 2011 Horseshoe Two and Monument fires, which occurred after the period for which we analyzed data, were much larger than any of the fires that occurred from 2006 through 2010. Based on preliminary information, federal agencies reported that these two fires burned more than 250,000 acres—more than twice the cumulative total of all significant human-caused wildland fires in the area during the previous 5 years.

---

[14]DOD did not provide fire size data for 13 fires occurring on its lands.

Figure 3: Location of Significant Human-Caused Wildland Fires in the Arizona Border Region, 2006-2010

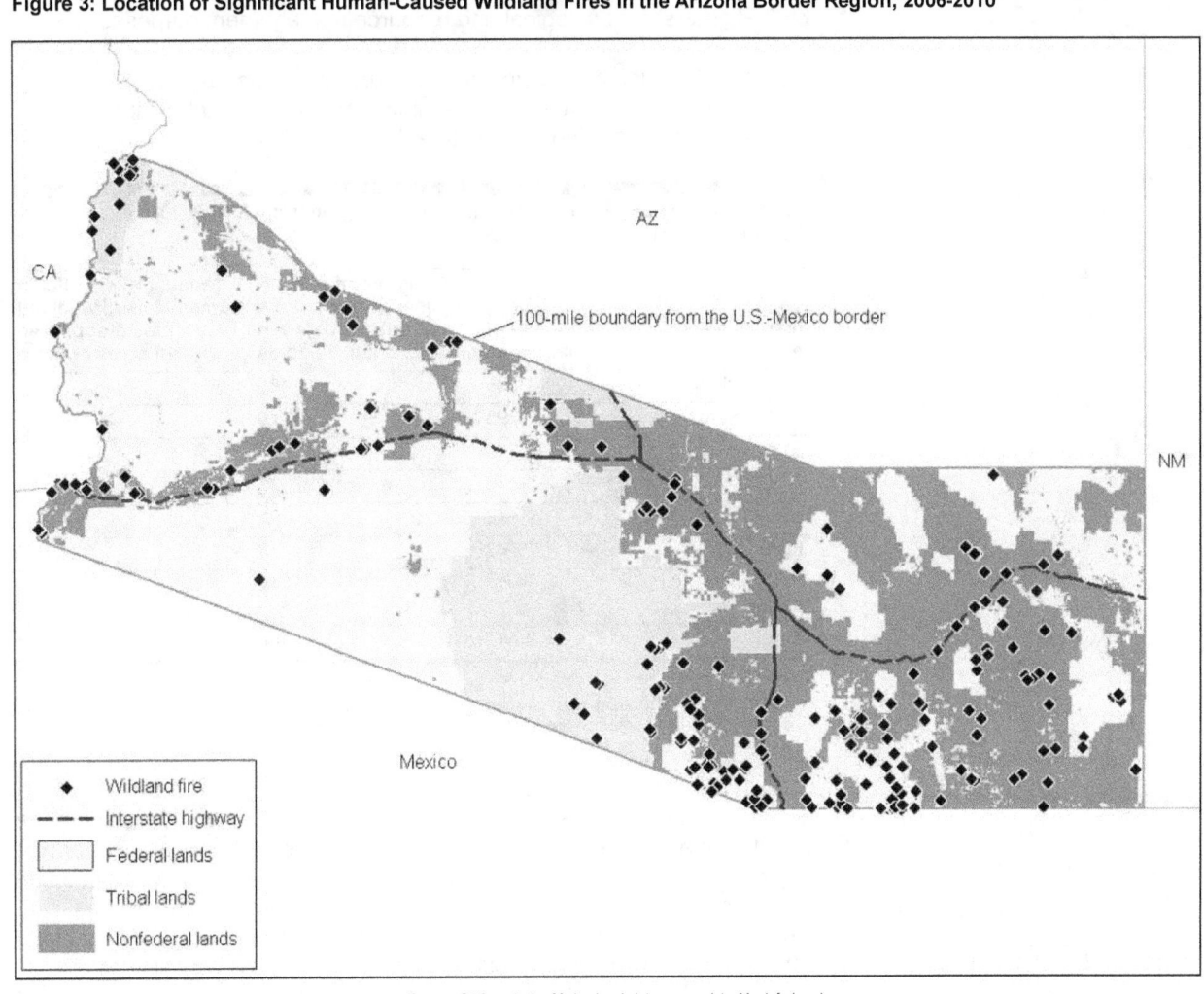

Source: GAO analysis of federal and state agency data; MapInfo (map).

Note: Significant human-caused wildland fires are those that burned 10 or more acres.

Of the 341 fires that federal and state agencies determined to be natural ignitions—caused by lightning—156, or 46 percent, burned less than 1 acre each; 87 burned from 1 to 10 acres each; and 98 fires were significant, burning 10 acres or more. Naturally ignited wildland fires burned nearly 74,000 acres, although agency officials explained that some of these fires were allowed to burn (i.e., they were not suppressed by firefighters) for ecological and resource management purposes.

Of the 2,467 wildland fires included in our review, the majority of the fires—1,553, or 63 percent—were ignited on federal or tribal lands. The remaining fires were ignited on state, local, or private lands (see table 1).

Table 1: Wildland Fires in the Arizona Border Region from 2006-2010, by Land Management Entity

Land management entity	Total number of wildland fires	Number of human-caused wildland fires that burned between 1 and 10 acres	Number of significant human-caused wildland fires that burned 10 acres or more
BIA/tr bal	558	180	28
Forest Service	395	49	71
BLM	340	28	37
DOD[a]	176	27	9
NPS	42	1	3
FWS	42	8	17
State, local, or private	914	215	76
Total	**2,467**	**508**	**241**

Source: GAO analysis of federal and state agency data.

[a]DOD data may not present a comprehensive account of wildland fires on DOD-managed lands. For example, DOD did not provide fire size data for 13 wildland fires.

The Economic and Environmental Effects of Significant Wildland Fires in the Arizona Border Region Are Not Fully Known

Significant human-caused wildland fires in the Arizona border region have resulted in a number of economic and environmental impacts. Economic impacts include millions of dollars in fire suppression costs, destruction of homes and ranching operations, and impacts on regional tourism. Environmental impacts include damaged habitat for endangered species and expansion of nonnative plants in the region. However, it is not possible to fully quantify the effects of these fires on the region's economy or environment because complete information needed for such analyses is not available.

Significant Human-Caused Wildland Fires Have Resulted in Various Economic Impacts, but the Full Impact on the Region Is Unknown

Significant human-caused wildland fires in the Arizona border region have had various economic impacts. These impacts include (1) the costs associated with suppressing wildland fires; (2) the destruction of property, including homes and ranching infrastructure; and (3) impacts on tourism. While we were able to identify specific examples of these fires' impacts on the area's economy, we could not determine the overall impact of these fires on local economies because complete information is not available that would allow such an analysis.

Fire suppression costs. In response to significant human-caused wildland fires that occurred from 2006 through 2010 in the Arizona border region, federal land management agencies obligated more than $33 million for suppression activities,[15] and the state of Arizona obligated almost $2 million.[16] Forest Service suppression obligations accounted for more than $26 million, or about 80 percent of all federal obligations to suppress these fires. The amount of funding obligated for individual significant human-caused wildland fires varied widely. For a majority of these fires, federal and state agencies obligated less than $25,000 per fire. Conversely, for 23 fires, or about 10 percent, agencies obligated more than $250,000 each, with the 2010 Horseshoe Fire, which burned more than 3,400 acres on the Coronado National Forest, accounting for more than $10 million—nearly a third of all federal obligations for significant human-caused wildland fires in the region from 2006 through 2010.[17] Characteristics affecting suppression costs include fire size; fuel types; fire intensity; physical terrain; proximity to the nearest community; total value of structures close to the fire; and special management

---

[15]The dollar values are as provided by the agencies and have not been adjusted for inflation. Based on preliminary information from the Forest Service and Department of the Interior, the 2011 Horseshoe Two and Monument fires together cost more than $70 million to suppress—twice the total reported federal and state obligations for suppressing all significant human-caused wildland fires from 2006 through 2010. However, as noted earlier, these fires occurred after the period of our data analysis and we have not independently assessed the validity of this cost information.

[16]These amounts do not include suppression cost data from DOD or local entities with fire management responsibilities, such as individual tribes, municipalities, or local fire protection districts. In addition, for those agencies that provided us with data, suppression costs can continue to be incurred several years after a fire occurrence; thus, our analysis may not include all fire suppression costs associated with these fires.

[17]See appendix II for detailed information on funding obligations, duration, and burned acreage associated with each significant human-caused wildland fire that occurred in the Arizona border region from 2006 through 2010.

considerations, such as whether the fire was burning in a wilderness or other designated area. It is also important to note that suppression costs may represent only a fraction of the total true costs for these fires. For example, one study that reviewed six fires of at least 40,000 acres in the western United States found that, in these cases, other costs associated with the fires, such as damage to properties and ecosystems and loss of economic activities, were generally several times higher than suppression costs.[18]

Destruction of property and injuries to homeowners. Significant human-caused wildland fires in the region have destroyed houses and other property and injured residents. For example, according to the Forest Service, the 2009 Canelo Fire, which burned over 4,000 acres, destroyed at least three residences, several outbuildings, and numerous vehicles. In addition, one homeowner was seriously burned during that wildland fire and required hospitalization. Similarly, the 2011 Monument Fire destroyed more than 60 homes, according to preliminary agency estimates.

Impacts on ranching operations. Significant human-caused wildland fires have also affected ranching operations in the region. Such fires have damaged grazing allotments and related improvements[19]—such as fences, water tanks, and pipelines—located on federal lands and used by private ranchers.[20] The Forest Service reported obligating more than $100,000 in long-term restoration and rehabilitation funds to repair fences, protect watersheds, and clean water tanks on federal grazing

---

[18]Western Forestry Leadership Coalition, *The True Cost of Wildfire in the Western U.S.* (April 2010).

[19]To provide access to grazing, both BLM and the Forest Service divide their rangelands into allotments, which can vary in size from a few acres to hundreds of thousands of acres of land. Because of the land ownership patterns that occurred when the lands were settled, the allotments can be adjacent to private lands, or they can be intermingled with private lands.

[20]For fires that occurred during 2011 (subsequent to the period of our data analysis), the Forest Service has reported preliminary estimates of at least $3.8 million in damage to federal grazing allotments, including from the Horseshoe Two Fire—which occurred on the Coronado National Forest. According to the Forest Service, the Horseshoe Two fire damaged approximately 120 miles of fence and destroyed at least 50 improvements, such as corrals, pipelines, water tanks, and wells.

allotments damaged by four significant human-caused wildland fires.[21] Additionally, from 2006 through 2010, Forest Service officials told us they provided about $56,000 in fencing and pipeline materials to repair damage on 15 allotments burned by significant human-caused wildland fires.[22] Forest Service officials told us the agency does not always have supplies to provide, however, and generally does not provide labor to repair damage to allotments. As a result, local ranchers can incur costs for labor and materials to repair damage to allotments. One rancher whose federal grazing allotment was burned during the 2009 Hog Fire told us that, although the Forest Service has offered to provide the materials to replace fencing that was burned during the fire, in order to use the allotment again, he would have to spend about $250,000 for labor costs to build the new fence to Forest Service specifications.

Additionally, federal agency officials and private ranchers told us that, in some circumstances, ranchers must move their cattle from federal grazing allotments because agencies have determined that the damage to the vegetation on which the cattle feed requires time to recover—typically 1 to 3 years, according to federal officials. As a result of significant human-caused wildland fires from 2006 through 2010, Forest Service officials reported that some cattle were removed from 20 allotments, and grazing schedules were altered for at least an additional 5, to allow vegetation to recover. A Forest Service official told us that the grazing capacity for 17 of these allotments has been reduced by 25 percent because of wildland fires. Additionally, one allotment that covers more than 50,000 acres was affected by 13 significant human-caused wildland fires from 2006 through 2010, according to federal agency officials, resulting in the repeated removal of cattle from the allotment and an altering of grazing schedules. According to industry representatives and private ranchers, moving cattle from an allotment negatively affects ranchers because they must either find alternative locations to graze their

---

[21]The Forest Service was the only agency that reported to us that it provided funds or materials to restore damaged rangeland improvements in response to significant human-caused wildland fires that occurred from 2006 through 2010. The Forest Service manages about 320 active federal grazing allotments in the Arizona border region.

[22]Another Forest Service official reported providing an additional $65,000 for fencing material for 2 additional allotments damaged by fire, and added that an additional 15 had been affected by wildland fires from 2006 through 2010—although this official could not determine how much of this damage resulted from significant human-caused wildland fires and how much resulted from fires that were smaller or naturally ignited.

cattle or purchase additional feed. Further, private ranchers stated that the value of their cattle can potentially decrease as a result of the stresses to the animals associated with the fires and transfers between allotments.

Impacts on tourism. Significant human-caused wildland fires can also affect tourism. According to a representative from the Cochise College Center for Economic Research,[23] as well as local residents that we spoke with, fires can affect tourism because access to trails, campgrounds, and roads can be temporarily restricted and, more broadly, fires can diminish the appeal of the region for tourists. For example, local residents told us that hospitality businesses in Portal, Arizona, have been particularly vulnerable to the economic impacts of wildland fires because these businesses are dependent on visitors to the Coronado National Forest. If access to the forest is restricted, as it was in 2010 as a result of the Horseshoe Fire, these residents told us it can have a direct impact on local businesses.

While the preceding examples provide some understanding of the nature of the economic impacts of significant human-caused wildland fires in the Arizona border region, we could not quantify the overall effect of these fires on the region because comprehensive and consistent data are not available. For example, we found no data that would allow us to determine the extent to which the closures of national forests and other public lands have affected tourism in the region, and we likewise did not find data that would allow us to identify the cumulative impact of significant human-caused wildland fires on tourist-related businesses.[24] Moreover, the economic researcher from the Cochise College Center for Economic Research noted that it is difficult to assess the overall economic impact of such incidents because the Arizona border region is rich in ecotourism resources. As a result, it is possible that visitors who could not visit a specific location may have still visited the region, simply choosing to visit other local areas. Additionally, as noted in one study we reviewed, identifying the real cost of wildland fires on the economy is

---

[23]Cochise County is one of four counties entirely within the Arizona border region. Five additional counties are partially within the region.

[24]The 2011 Horseshoe Two Fire did require the evacuation of Portal for several days, causing businesses in the community to close, but the precise economic effect of the evacuation on the region is likewise unknown.

difficult because few data sources are consistent from fire to fire, and many lack any data at all.[25] According to this study, the effects resulting from individual fires are unique to each fire and cannot be generally extrapolated to other fires. The representative we spoke to from the Cochise College Center for Economic Research also noted that the economic effects of wildland fire can be mixed and, therefore, difficult to delineate. For example, while wildland fires can provide a temporary boost to several industries in the region—such as construction and retail and restaurant sales—that boost could be offset by increases in home insurance premiums in the area and lost revenue and wages from other displaced businesses or workers.

Significant Human-Caused Wildland Fires Have Damaged the Environment, but the Full Extent Is Unknown

Significant human-caused wildland fires have damaged the natural environment in the Arizona border region, but the comprehensive effects are unknown, in part because—as with the economic effects of wildland fires—complete information is not available on the environmental effects of wildland fire. According to our analysis of federal emergency treatment plans and discussions with federal agency and tribal officials, the most common environmental effects of wildland fire in the region are expansion of nonnative plant species, degraded endangered species habitat, and soil erosion. These effects may result from both significant human-caused wildland fires and other fires. The following are descriptions of these environmental effects and examples of the effects that have been noted from individual instances of significant human-caused wildland fires in the region.[26]

Expansion of nonnative plant species. Plant species that are not native to southern Arizona, such as buffelgrass and tamarisk—commonly known as salt cedar—can regenerate more quickly following wildland fires than native species and may displace such species from their traditional ranges. The expansion of these species can also alter natural fire patterns by making areas susceptible to burning with more severity or frequency than they traditionally would. For example, the 2009 Powers

---

[25]Dennis L. Lynch, "What Do Forest Fires Really Cost?," *Journal of Forestry* (September 2004).

[26]As we have reported, wildland fire can have dramatic positive and negative environmental effects. See GAO, *Wildland Fires: Forest Service and BLM Need Better Information and a Systematic Approach for Assessing the Risks of Environmental Effects*, GAO-04-705 (Washington, D.C.: June 24, 2004).

Fire, a human-caused wildland fire that burned 260 acres, destroyed native vegetation such as cottonwood and willows along the Gila River. As a result, BLM predicts that nonnative salt cedar will increase in density along the river. BLM noted in its postwildfire environmental damage assessment that the increased density of salt cedar will degrade the habitat because salt cedar actively resprouts after wildland fires and can create enough fuel to burn again within 5 years.

Damage to endangered species habitat. Southern Arizona is home to a number of federally listed threatened and endangered plant and animal species.[27] Some wildland fires can damage the habitats of these species and, in turn, threaten their continued existence. For example, the 2007 San Luis Fire—a human-caused wildland fire that burned 68 acres of mostly BLM land—damaged riparian areas that are habitat for two bird species federally listed as endangered, the Southwestern Willow Flycatcher and the Yuma Clapper Rail, as well as another that is a candidate for listing, the Yellow-Billed Cuckoo.[28]

Increased soil erosion. Soil erosion can also result from wildland fires in the region. During the seasonal "monsoon rains" that Arizona typically experiences in the summer, areas where wildland fires have burned away the vegetation holding soil together may experience increased runoff and mudslides that can damage natural habitats, watersheds, roads, and trails. For example, an official with the Tohono O'odham Nation told us that the nation is concerned about the impact the human-caused 2009 Elkhorn Fire will have on the Kearney's Blue Star, which is an endangered plant species. The fire itself did not damage the plant's population, but as a result of the fire, water runoff and soil erosion are expected to increase, which would threaten the plant's population at lower elevations.

To mitigate such impacts on federal lands in the region, from 2006 through 2010, federal agencies obligated nearly $1.9 million through the Burned Area Emergency Response program—a federal program that

---

[27]The Endangered Species Act of 1973 protects plant and animal species that are either facing extinction (endangered species) or are likely to face extinction in the foreseeable future (threatened species) and protects the ecosystems upon which they depend.

[28]Riparian areas—the narrow bands of green vegetation along the banks of rivers and streams—are widely recognized as crucial to the overall ecological health of rangelands.

provides funds to stabilize and prevent degradation to natural and cultural resources resulting from the effects of wildland fires. Agencies prioritize and fund emergency treatments based on risks identified in damage assessments. According to Forest Service guidance, Burned Area Emergency Response program assessments should be conducted for fires that burn more than 300 acres, though damage from smaller fires can be assessed if federal land management agency officials believe that life, property, or damage to natural or cultural resources are at risk. From 2006 through 2010, federal agencies assessed damage from 20 significant human-caused wildland fires in the Arizona border region for emergency treatment funding under this program. Based on these assessments, federal officials recommended that funds be used to provide emergency treatment in response to damage from 9 of these fires and approved at least partial funding for 7 of these fires. For 10 of the 11 assessed fires for which they did not recommend emergency treatment funding, officials believed that the damaged areas would recover naturally in 5 years or less without any treatment program.

The above examples provide some understanding of the types of environmental effects of significant human caused wildland fires in the Arizona border region, but we were unable to quantify the full environmental impacts for the region because comprehensive information is not available. For example, according to federal agency officials, the amount of funding provided through the Burned Area Emergency Response program reflects only a portion of the total monetary value of the environmental damages resulting from significant human-caused wildland fires, in part because not all such fires receive funding under the program. In addition, federal officials told us that many of the significant human-caused wildland fires that have occurred in the Arizona border region have likely resulted in at least some environmental damage, but these effects are generally not formally documented or recorded by federal agencies, and often it is many years before the extent of the damage is fully evident. Similarly, state agencies such as the Arizona State Forestry Division and the Arizona State Land Department could not provide us with data regarding the environmental consequences of significant human-caused wildland fires that occurred on state lands because, according to state officials, they do not maintain such data.

Federal Agencies Did Not Conduct Investigations of All Human-Caused Wildland Fires and Thus Cannot Determine the Number Ignited by Illegal Border Crossers

The frequency with which illegal border crossers have caused wildland fires on federal lands in the Arizona border region is not fully known, in part because federal land management agencies did not conduct investigations of all human-caused wildland fires that occurred on their lands as called for by interagency policy. Further, the fires that were investigated—about 18 percent of the fires we examined (77 of 422 fires)—were selected for investigation based primarily on the availability of fire investigators, according to agency officials, rather than on the specific characteristics of the fires, such as their size or location. Without more information on the specific causes of these fires, the agencies lack key data that could help them target their fire prevention efforts.

Federal Agencies Did Not Conduct Investigations of All Human-Caused Wildland Fires As Called for by Interagency Policy

Federal agencies cannot identify all of the human-caused wildland fires that were ignited by illegal border crossers on federal lands, in part because they did not conduct the investigations called for by interagency policy. This policy—*Interagency Standards for Fire and Fire Aviation Operations*, which applies to the Forest Service, BLM, FWS, and NPS— calls for these agencies to determine the general cause—human or natural—for all wildland fires on federal lands they manage.[29] If a wildland fire is determined to be human-caused, the interagency policy calls for a more in-depth investigation to be conducted, typically by personnel trained to conduct fire cause investigations. Similarly, the *Wildland Fire and Aviation Program Management Operations Guide*, which applies to BIA, also calls for thorough cause investigations for all wildland fires suspected to be human caused.

---

[29]DOD is not a signatory to this policy and does not generally conduct investigations into the causes of wildland fires on its properties. As a result, we did not include the agency in our analysis.

There were 422 human-caused wildland fires that burned 1 or more acres on federal or tribal lands between 2006 and 2010.[30] Of these, federal fire investigators conducted investigations for 77—or about 18 percent. Table 2 and figure 4 provide additional information on the fires investigated.

Table 2: Number of Wildland Fires Investigated, by Agency, 2006-2010

Land management agency	Human-caused wildland fires that burned 1 or more acres		
	Number of fires	Number investigated	Percentage investigated
BIA/tribal[a]	208	1	<1
Forest Service	120	57	48
BLM	65	7	11
NPS	4	2	50
FWS	25	10	40
Total	422	77	18

Source: GAO analysis of Forest Service and Interior data.

[a]Wildland fires occurring on Tohono O'odham tribal land are included in the BIA total. The Tohono O'odham Nation has assumed responsibility for wildland fire suppression and investigation responsibilities, under the Indian Self-Determination and Education Assistance Act, as amended.

Officials from the Forest Service, BIA, BLM, and FWS told us that the primary reason that many human-caused wildland fires were not investigated was because the agencies lacked available trained fire investigators. For example, both BLM and Forest Service officials told us the agency's law enforcement officers, who are trained to conduct such investigations, do not have the time to investigate all human-caused wildland fires because of other responsibilities, such as providing security for firefighters and their equipment. Similarly, an official from the Tohono O'odham Nation stated that, although he believes it is important to determine the cause of these fires, the nation's fire management program does not have adequate funding to support a wildland fire investigator.

---

[30]These 422 fires include those that occurred on Forest Service, BIA, BLM, NPS, FWS, or tribal land. Given the elevated level of wildland fire activity that occurred during the 2011 fire season in the Arizona border region, we limited our analysis to human-caused wildland fires burning 1 acre or more, rather than all human-caused fires, in order to obtain data needed for this review without creating an unreasonable burden for fire and law enforcement officials providing us with the data. We also did not include the 36 human-caused wildland fires that burned 1 or more acres on DOD land in the Arizona border region. See appendix I for more information on our methodology.

This official also stated that he has requested assistance from federal agencies to investigate some fires, but the agencies have been unable to provide such assistance because of other priorities.

The lack of fire investigations is not a recent issue. A 1998 Department of the Interior Inspector General report found weaknesses with the agency's ability to investigate fires, stating that seven of the eight BLM district offices reviewed by the Inspector General did not give sufficient priority to fire investigations and did not adequately document the fire investigations that were completed.[31] Even for those fires that are investigated, federal officials told us a decision on whether to investigate a fire is generally not based on the specific characteristics of the fire, such as its size or location. Rather, they said the decision generally depends on the availability of a trained wildland fire investigator at the time of the fire. Although it appears the agencies have concluded they cannot investigate all fires because they do not have sufficient resources, they have not developed a strategy for determining which fires to investigate. Such a strategy could include specific criteria for identifying which fires to investigate, such as fires that are larger than average, that stand to burn sensitive areas, or that otherwise may have effects that make their origins important to understand. Without such a strategy, the agencies are unable to ensure that those human-caused wildland fires with the greatest effects are consistently investigated.

---

[31]BLM, *Reimbursement of Firefighting Costs, Bureau of Land Management*, 98-I-551 (Washington, D.C.: July 1998).

Federal Fire Investigators Identified Illegal Border Crossers as a Suspected Cause of Ignition in 30 of the 77 Fires They Investigated

Based on our review of agency investigation reports, illegal border crossers were a suspected cause of ignition for 30 of the 77 investigated wildland fires, or about 39 percent.[32] Five of the 30 wildland fires in which illegal border crossers were a suspected cause burned less than 10 acres each, 16 burned from 10 to 100 acres each, and 9 burned more than 100 acres each. These 30 wildland fires were all located within 40 miles of the U.S.-Mexico border and occurred on the Coronado National Forest, Buenos Aires National Wildlife Refuge, or Organ Pipe Cactus National Monument (see fig. 4 for the location of wildland fires that occurred on federal lands and which illegal border crossers were identified as a suspected cause).

---

[32]Some investigations resulted in the identification of more than one potential ignition source, meaning that the total number of suspected ignition sources is greater than the total number of fires investigated.

Figure 4: Wildland Fires on Federal Lands for Which Agency Investigation Reports Identified Illegal Border Crossers as a Suspected Ignition Source

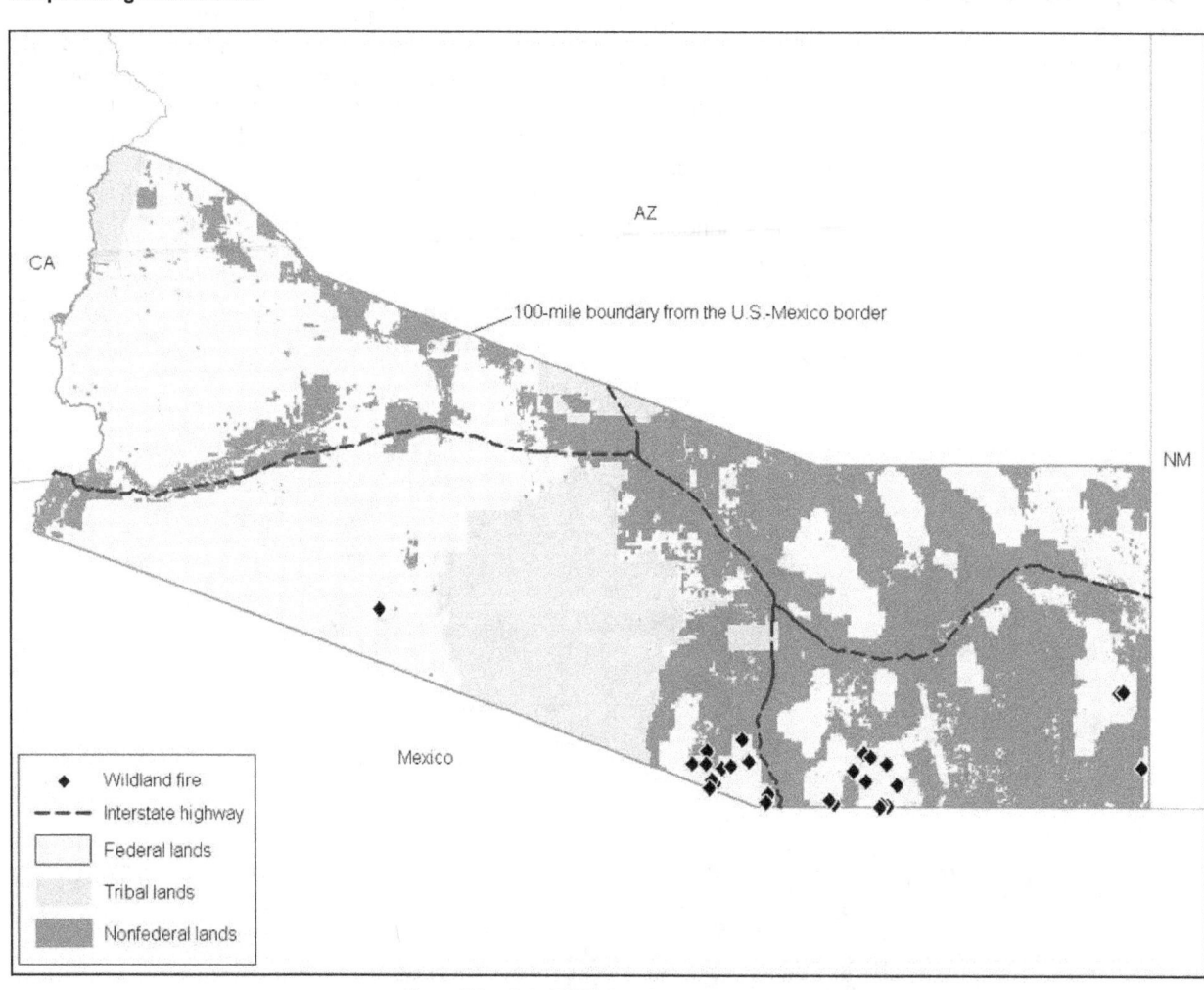

Source: GAO analysis of USDA's Forest Service and Interior agencies' fire investigation reports; MapInfo (map).

Investigation reports identified illegal border crossers as a suspected cause of 15 wildland fires that resulted from efforts to signal for help, provide warmth, or cook food. For example, the investigation report for the 2006 Black Mesa Fire, which burned about 170 acres, states that the wildland fire was ignited because a border crosser was injured and needed assistance. According to the report, a group of about 20 individuals crossed illegally into the United States and, during the trip, one person was injured and could not continue. The group continued without the injured person, but first started a fire to keep animals away and to attract attention in the hope that someone would rescue the injured person. In another instance—the 2009 Bear Fire, which burned 15 acres—the investigation report states that a campfire was the probable cause, noting several indicators regarding a potential source of ignition: (1) discarded bottles and food wrappers with Spanish language labels were found in the area of origin; (2) the area is frequented by illegal border crossers and is adjacent to a heavily used smuggling trail; and (3) the fire was ignited at a time when illegal border crossers are often known to travel.

The investigation reports for the remaining 15 wildland fires suspected to be ignited by illegal border crossers did not explicitly indicate a purpose for the ignition, though a couple of investigation reports for these fires noted that the area of ignition is known for drug smuggling. For instance, the investigation report for the 2010 Horseshoe Fire, which burned about 3,400 acres, stated that evidence found during the investigation suggests that drug smugglers were in the area of ignition.[33]

For the other investigated human-caused wildland fires that were not linked to illegal border crossers, federal agency investigation reports identified a number of other potential human causes that could have caused the ignition, and in some cases the investigation reports did not identify any specific cause. Examples from investigation reports include the following:

- Resident campfires were a suspected source of 13 wildland fires, including the 2009 Carr Link Fire, where a visitor to the Coronado National Forest was suspected of leaving a campsite for a day hike without properly extinguishing the campfire.

- Other activities such as recreational shooting, welding accidents, sparks from all-terrain vehicles, and fireworks were a suspected source of 25 fires, such as the 2009 Mile Post 6 Fire on the Coronado

---

[33]The 2011 Horseshoe Two Fire was not included as part of our analysis and is not reflected in our overall number of fires suspected to be caused by illegal border crossers. However, the investigation report for the fire was completed in June 2011 and stated the area of origin had no reported lightning strikes, the use of motor vehicles in the area was not probable, and the area was not known to be used by recreational campers. The investigation report also documents that camping fires used to keep warm are common in the area of origin due to the volume of illegal border crossers who travel through the region.

National Forest, where target shooters shot rocks and sparks from the bullets ignited dry grass; and the 2007 San Antonio Fire, where a resident accidentally ignited the fire while welding.

- Investigation reports indicate that investigators could not determine a cause or did not document a suspected cause for 17 fires. These wildland fires ranged in size from 1 acre to 5,070 acres.

To obtain additional information on possible causes of wildland fires, we also reviewed fire incident reports for the 1,123 human-caused wildland fires that occurred on federal and tribal land in the region from 2006 through 2010. Fire incident reports are distinct from investigation reports in that they are completed for each wildland fire and contain overall information on the fires' size, location, and general cause, but they are not formal investigations into the fire's origin. In addition to collecting general fire information, these incident reports allow firefighters to include comments regarding their views on the fires' causes—although such comments are not mandatory and firefighters completing the fire incident reports often choose not to include this kind of information. Of the fire incident reports we reviewed, 57 included firefighter comments noting illegal border crossers as a suspected cause of the fire. Most of these (32 of the 57) were for wildland fires that occurred on the Tohono O'odham tribal land. According to a tribal official, illegal border crossers are a significant cause of wildland fires on tribal land and the purpose of the fires is usually to signal for assistance, cook food, or to provide warmth. Appendix III includes additional information about the fire incident reports we reviewed and a map identifying the location of the 57 wildland fires.

Without Comprehensive Fire Investigation Results, Federal Agencies Lack Key Data Needed to Target Their Fire Prevention Efforts

Without complete data on the cause of wildland fires on the lands that they manage, federal agencies are hampered in their ability to target their efforts and resources at preventing future wildland fires. According to interagency guidance, the *Wildfire Origin and Cause Determination Handbook*, identifying trends in fire causes is critical to the success of fire prevention programs, and the results of fire investigations can assist in policy development. Similarly, a Forest Service document states that the first step in the prevention of human-caused wildland fires is to determine the group most likely to start fires. However, in reviewing several agency fire prevention plans for the region, we found that they included only broad wildland fire awareness programs and activities but did not identify specific trends or discuss groups likely to start fires or discuss the possible role of illegal border crossers in contributing to fires in the region. Without either additional data on the ignition source of fires in the Arizona border region or a systematic process for using the information identified in investigation reports, it will be difficult for the land management agencies to identify more specific wildland fire prevention activities or better target fire prevention efforts and resources.

In contrast, the experience of the Cleveland National Forest in California provides an example of the potential benefits of better targeting fire prevention efforts. In 1996, the Forest Service formed the Border Agency Fire Council in Southern California to help identify activities that could prevent future wildland fires.[34] Using data on the cause of wildland fires, the council determined that a number of wildland fires were the result of improperly extinguished campfires left by illegal border crossers. In response, officials from the Cleveland National Forest created a border fire prevention crew that hikes daily on trails known to be used by illegal border crossers and extinguishes abandoned campfires. In 2008 alone, the forest reported that the fire prevention crew extinguished 101 abandoned campfires that, had they not been suppressed, could have grown into larger and more damaging wildland fires. This example demonstrates that with better information about the specific ignition source of human-caused wildland fires, the agencies could be better equipped to take actions that may prevent future wildland fires.

The Presence of Illegal Border Crossers Has Complicated Fire Suppression Activities, and Agencies' Responses May Not Fully Address the Issue

The presence of illegal border crossers has increased the complexity of fire suppression activities in the border region, according to federal agency officials, because it can endanger firefighters' safety, complicate the use of radio communications, and limit the use of certain types of fire suppression activities. Agencies have taken a number of actions to mitigate the threats to firefighters in the Arizona border region, but these actions may not be sufficient to ensure that agency resources are being used most effectively, and none of the agencies has developed a risk-based approach for using resources to support fire suppression activities in the region.

---

[34]The Border Agency Fire Council is made up of 43 U.S. and Mexican government agencies and organizations representing fire protection and law enforcement personnel, legislators, emergency responders, natural resource managers, and elected officials that address public safety issues pertaining to wildland fire along the U.S.-Mexico border.

The Presence of Illegal Border Crossers Has Complicated Wildland Fire Suppression Activities in the Arizona Border Region

The presence of illegal border crossers has complicated wildland fire suppression activities in the Arizona border region, according to federal agency officials, largely because of concerns about firefighter safety. In 2006, the Forest Service issued a report stating that the Arizona border region is made more dangerous for firefighters because they may encounter smugglers; high-speed law enforcement pursuits; environments littered with trash and other biological hazards; and illegal border crossers who are seeking food, water, transportation, or rescue.[35] While federal agency officials we interviewed, including fire response and law enforcement officials, did not identify any specific incidents in which firefighters had been assaulted or threatened by illegal border crossers, they identified several aspects of illegal cross-border activity that firefighters must account for while suppressing fires in the region.

Firefighters may encounter armed smugglers. Federal agency officials told us that violence could result if firefighters encounter armed smugglers while suppressing fires in remote areas. They did not provide any examples of specific situations in which firefighters had experienced such violent encounters with smugglers; however, officials cited instances in which individuals they believed to be illegal border crossers were encountered during fire suppression activities. The fire investigation report for the recent 2011 Horseshoe Two Fire indicates that drug smugglers continued to use that area even as fire suppression activities were underway.

Illegal border crossers may be injured or killed by suppression activities. A number of fire response officials told us that they believe many illegal border crossers generally try to avoid contact with firefighters in the region—which, while reducing concern for firefighters' safety, raises concerns about the safety of illegal border crossers who could be harmed or killed by fire suppression activities. For example, firefighters sometimes set backfires—the burning of grass, leaves, brush, and other fuels located between an advancing fire and an established control line, such as a road—to halt the spread of wildland fires. Given the concern about the possible presence of illegal border crossers in the Arizona border region, firefighters—or, in some cases, U.S. Border Patrol agents—will, in some instances, first conduct a search of an area to attempt to identify whether

---

[35]Lisa Outka-Perkins, Theron Miller, and Jon Driessen; USDA Forest Service and Missoula Technology and Development Center; *Personal Safety of Federal Land-Management Field Employees Working Along the Mexican Border;* 0067-2802-MTDC (2006).

illegal border crossers are in harm's way before igniting a backfire. This additional step can increase the resources and time needed to suppress the fire.[36]

Firefighters may reduce their use of nighttime firefighting activities. The potential presence of illegal border crossers has caused agencies to reduce their use of nighttime fire suppression activities and temporary overnight camps for firefighters because of the perceived threat to firefighters' safety. As a result, firefighters may have to forgo or delay some firefighting tactics, which in turn may allow fires to grow larger and more damaging. For example, a Forest Service official told us that on the first day of the 2009 Hog Fire, firefighters were unable to set up an overnight camp at the scene of the fire because no law enforcement support was available to provide security. According to this official, this allowed the fire, which had burned 200 to 300 acres at the time, to grow to more than 3,000 acres by the next morning; the fire ultimately burned nearly 17,000 acres and cost more than $700,000 to suppress.

Illegal cross-border activity may interfere with radio communications. According to agency officials from several land management agencies, communicating by radio is difficult as a result of illegal cross-border activity in the Arizona border region. For example, according to federal agency and tribal officials, illegal border crossers may use the same radio frequencies as firefighters, causing interference and limiting their ability to safely coordinate fire suppression activities. In one instance, a tribal official told us that the Tohono O'odham Nation's sole radio repeater—which allows firefighters to communicate over long distances—had its frequency taken over by illegal border crossers and is now unusable to firefighters.[37] The tribal official stated that the lack of access to a repeater limits firefighters' ability to communicate. We were also told by Forest Service officials that firefighters are instructed not to use radios when they encounter illegal border crossers because illegal border crossers may

---

[36]According to Border Patrol and federal land management agency officials, Border Patrol agents do not generally participate in wildland fire suppression activities. However, in some situations, they may provide certain types of assistance during these activities, such as providing temporary security for firefighters until federal land management agency law enforcement can arrive.

[37]Radio repeaters are used to increase the effective communications range of handheld portable radios, mobile radios, and base station radios by retransmitting received radio signals.

believe that firefighters are reporting their location to law enforcement and react violently.

Volume of air traffic increases the importance of interagency coordination. According to federal and tribal officials, aerial fire suppression activities in the Arizona border region require extra caution because of the high volume of other federal air traffic in the area—particularly DHS aircraft conducting border security operations, such as drug interdiction or search and rescue, and DOD aircraft conducting training flights. According to the officials, both fire suppression and DHS aircraft often operate at low altitude and in the same areas along the border, making the risk of a midair collision higher than in other areas across the country. To enhance safety, they emphasize the importance of coordinating with agency dispatch centers to ensure that airspace is clear of other traffic when conducting aerial fire suppression activities.

Firefighters may be distracted by the presence of illegal border crossers. More broadly, officials from several land management agencies told us the potential presence of illegal border crossers is a distraction to firefighters that can result in firefighters focusing more on their own security, or that of illegal border crossers, than on suppressing the fire. In addition, agency officials stated that firefighters have discovered the bodies of illegal border crossers, which further distracts them and affects their morale.

Agencies Have Taken Steps to Mitigate Threats to Firefighters in the Arizona Border Region but Do Not Have a Formal Risk-Based Approach for Using Their Resources

The Forest Service has taken a number of actions to mitigate the threats to firefighters' safety in the Arizona border region—which other agencies have generally followed. In 2008, the Forest Service published an instructional DVD to educate federal, state, local, and tribal employees working along the U.S.-Mexico border on safety concerns and work practices that can reduce on-the-job risks.[38] One of the training modules specifically discusses illegal border crossers' effects on fire suppression activities in the region and special precautions that firefighters should take. The Forest Service also produces and distributes "International Border Watchouts" cards to all firefighters conducting suppression activities on the Coronado National Forest. These cards highlight specific

---

[38]USDA Forest Service and Missoula Technology and Development Center, *Working Along the United States-Mexico Border*, 0823-2M29-MTDC (2008).

risks that firefighters might face when suppressing fires on the forest and include a map identifying where—based on proximity to the border—they are most likely to encounter these risks.

The Forest Service has also developed a Border Fire Response Protocol, which recommends that firefighters working in the Arizona border region consider taking certain actions to mitigate the potential risks posed by illegal cross-border activity. One of the recommended actions is for fire responders to request that law enforcement support be dispatched to fires in the region to provide security for firefighters and their equipment. Officials from all five federal land management agencies explained that law enforcement provides security in multiple ways, including providing an armed presence while firefighters are suppressing fires or camping overnight, clearing areas of any illegal border crossers that might be hiding in an area where fire suppression activities—such as backfires— are going to occur, and guarding fire suppression vehicles and equipment to prevent theft.

Officials from all of the other federal land management agencies in the region—BIA, BLM, FWS, and NPS—told us they generally follow the Forest Service's fire response protocol informally but that they have neither formally adopted it nor developed their own guidance to account for the impacts that illegal border crossers have on wildland fire suppression activities in the region. A number of federal officials in the border region from these agencies identified the lack of formal protocols for the four Interior land management agencies as a major concern, in part because without formal policies it is unclear that these agencies will provide the most appropriate and consistent fire response actions for the region. Under the *Standards for Internal Control in the Federal Government*, agencies are to employ control activities, which are the policies, procedures, techniques, and mechanisms to ensure effective program management and help ensure that actions are taken to avoid risk.[39] In this case, such activities would include protocols for federal land management agencies responding to wildland fires in the region.

More broadly, the land management agencies have recognized risks associated with fighting wildland fires in the Arizona border region, but

International Border Watchouts Card Provided to Firefighters by the Forest Service

International Border Watchouts!

1. Expect high speed driving and law enforcement pursuits
2. Expect drivers to be distracted
3. All aircraft operations have increased collision risk
4. Radio frequency interference from Mexico likely
5. Radio/cell phone dead spots increase employee risks
6. Cell phone connections to Mexico likely
7. Language barriers increase risk
8. Threats to employees are present 24/7/365
9. You are not clearly identified as F.S. employee
10. Every visitor contact has potential risk
11. Higher occurrence of unexpected visitor encounters
12. Traditional responses may not be appropriate, check your gut
13. Responding to situations inconsistent with assigned authority and training
14. Night operations require special considerations
15. Unattended vehicles will be damaged or stolen
16. Illegal uses in remote areas likely
17. Heightened risk of biological contamination
18. Always know your location and be able to describe it
19. Let others know your expected route and destination (checkin/check-out)

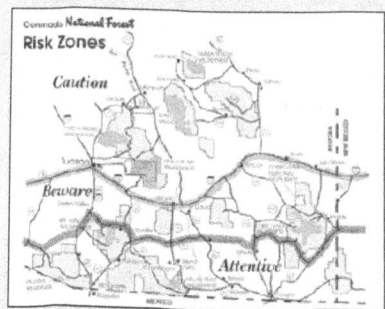

Source: USDA's Forest Service.

[39]GAO, *Standards for Internal Control in the Federal Government*, GAO/AIMD-00-21.3.1 (Washington, D.C.: November 1999).

none of the agencies use a risk-based approach for allocating law enforcement resources in support of wildland fire suppression activities specific to the region. Instead, law enforcement is dispatched to most wildland fires whether any specific threats have been identified or not. Both federal fire response and law enforcement officials told us that not all fire suppression activities need security because the threat posed to firefighters by illegal border crossers varies by fire. Further, fire response officials told us that waiting for law enforcement to arrive can delay firefighting efforts; similarly, law enforcement officials told us that being dispatched to all fires regardless of the level of safety concerns has hampered their ability to do other high-priority work, such as conducting drug interdiction or fire investigations. We have previously recommended that, when making decisions about needed law enforcement resources and how to distribute those resources, federal land management agencies should adopt a risk management approach to systematically assess and address threats and vulnerabilities.[40] This recommendation, which the agencies agreed with, noted that, in keeping with the *Standards for Internal Control in the Federal Government,* such an approach should identify risks, assess their magnitude and likelihood of occurrence, and use information from these assessments in determining the law enforcement resources needed and the best way to distribute those resources. However, such an approach has not been developed or implemented for the Arizona border region. Without a systematic risk-based approach that incorporates a consideration of the threats associated with individual fires, the agencies lack assurance that they are using their limited law enforcement resources in the most efficient manner.

Conclusions

Federal land management agencies in the Arizona border region face a set of complex and diverse challenges in carrying out their responsibilities, including those posed by illegal border crossers and wildland fires. In general, the agencies are well aware of the threats associated with wildland fire suppression activities in the border region and have taken some steps to address them, such as following the Forest Service's Border Fire Response Protocol. However, gaps in information and inefficient deployment of limited law enforcement resources create operational challenges limiting the agencies' ability to fully address the complications they face. The agencies do not have in-depth information

---

[40]GAO-11-144.

about the specific ignition sources of human-caused wildland fires in part because they have not conducted investigations for all human-caused fires—often because of limited resources—as called for by interagency policy. In a time of constrained resources and competing needs, we recognize that investigating all human-caused wildland fires in the Arizona border region may not be feasible. However, the agencies have not developed a strategy for determining which fires to investigate, including specific criteria to help identify and prioritize those fire incidents that should be investigated. Further, agencies do not have a systematic process for using the information identified in the investigations to inform decisions on prevention efforts. Without this information, it will be difficult for agency efforts to target fire prevention activities and resources and potentially reduce the incidence of human-caused wildland fires in the region. Further, the practice of dispatching law enforcement support to most fires, rather than considering the risk or safety concerns associated with individual fires, may delay fire suppression activities and prevent law enforcement from conducting other high-priority work, such as drug interdictions or fire investigations. Without a systematic risk-based approach that incorporates a consideration of the risks associated with individual fires, the agencies lack assurance that they are using their limited law enforcement resources in the most efficient manner. Finally, the Interior agencies have taken an important step by informally following the Border Fire Response Protocol developed by the Forest Service, but without formally adopting the protocol or developing corresponding protocols of their own, they lessen the chances that the procedures in the protocol will be consistently followed.

Recommendations for Executive Action

We recommend that the following five actions be taken:

- To ensure agencies have the data needed to identify wildland fire prevention activities and to ensure resources are effectively targeted, the Secretaries of Agriculture and the Interior should direct the Chief of the Forest Service, the Directors of the Bureau of Land Management, Fish and Wildlife Service, and National Park Service, and the Assistant Secretary for Indian Affairs to take the following actions: (1) re-examine the policy that all human-caused wildland fires be investigated; (2) once the agencies have determined the appropriate level of investigations, develop a strategy for determining which fires to investigate, including specific criteria to help select and prioritize those fire incidents that should be investigated; and (3) develop a systematic process to use the information identified in the investigations to better target fire prevention activities and resources.

- To ensure that fire suppression activities are not unnecessarily delayed and that law enforcement resources are efficiently allocated, the Secretaries of Agriculture and the Interior should direct the Chief of the Forest Service and the Directors of the Bureau of Land Management, Fish and Wildlife Service, and National Park Service to develop a coordinated risk-based approach for the region to determine when law enforcement support is warranted for each wildland fire occurrence and adjust their response procedures accordingly. In developing this approach, officials in the region should consult with agencies' headquarters to ensure consistency in the approaches being developed for the region and for all land management agency units nationwide.

- The Secretary of the Interior should direct the Directors of the Bureau of Land Management, Fish and Wildlife Service, and National Park Service, and the Assistant Secretary for Indian Affairs to develop border-specific fire response guidance or review existing guidance to determine whether it is sufficient and, if so, formally adopt it.

Agency Comments and Our Evaluation

We provided the Departments of Agriculture, Defense, Homeland Security, and the Interior with a draft of this report for their review and comment.

In its written comments, the Forest Service, responding on behalf of the Department of Agriculture, agreed with our observations and the two recommendations addressed to the agency. The Forest Service's comments are reproduced in appendix IV.

The Department of the Interior did not provide written comments to include in our report. However, in an e-mail received October 24, 2011, the agency liaison stated that Interior generally concurred with our recommendations and that implementing the recommendations will require consultation with the Department of Agriculture to ensure interagency consistency. Regarding our second recommendation, Interior noted that it disagrees that there is a lack of coordinated risk-based law enforcement support, but concurred that improvements and adjustments can be made. While we are encouraged that Interior acknowledges improvements can be made, based on our observations we continue to believe that the agency does not use a systematic risk-based approach that incorporates a consideration of the risks associated with individual fires when allocating law enforcement resources. Interior also noted that it agrees that coordination and consultation within the region and across the

GAO-12-73 Wildland Fire in the Arizona Border Region

nation for both responses with wildland fire and law enforcement in a refined risk-based approach can ensure that appropriate fire suppression responses are implemented. Interior also provided technical comments in its e-mail response, which we have incorporated as appropriate.

In its written comments, the Department of Homeland Security agreed with our observations about the complex and diverse challenges that federal land management agencies face in the Arizona border region. The department's comments are reproduced in appendix V.

The Department of Defense did not provide written or technical comments in response to our report.

As agreed with your offices, unless you publicly announce the contents of this report earlier, we plan no further distribution until 30 days from the report date. At that time, we will send copies to the Secretaries of Agriculture, Defense, Homeland Security, and the Interior; the Chief of the Forest Service; the Assistant Secretary for Indian Affairs; the Directors of the Bureau of Land Management, Fish and Wildlife Service, and National Park Service; appropriate congressional committees; and other interested parties. In addition, the report will be available at no charge on the GAO website at http://www.gao.gov.

If you or your staffs have questions about this report, please contact me at (202) 512-3841 or mittala@gao.gov. Contact points for our Offices of Congressional Relations and Public Affairs may be found on the last page of this report. Key contributors to this report are listed in appendix VI.

Anu K. Mittal
Director, Natural Resources and Environment

List of Requesters

The Honorable Lisa Murkowski
Ranking Member
Committee on Energy
  and Natural Resources
United States Senate

The Honorable John Barrasso
Ranking Member
Subcommittee on Public Lands
  and Forests
Committee on Energy and
  Natural Resources
United States Senate

The Honorable John McCain
United States Senate

The Honorable Jon Kyl
United States Senate

Appendix I: Scope and Methodology

The objectives of our review were to determine (1) the number, cause, size, and location of wildland fires in Arizona that occurred within 100 miles of the U.S.-Mexico border from 2006 through 2010; (2) economic and environmental effects of significant human-caused wildland fires (i.e., those fires that burned 10 or more acres); (3) the extent to which federal agencies determined that illegal border crossers were the ignition source of fires on federal lands; and (4) ways, if any, in which the presence of illegal border crossers has affected fire suppression activities in the Arizona border region.

To determine the extent of wildland fire occurrence in the Arizona border region, we collected federal and state fire occurrence data from databases at the National Interagency Fire Center (NIFC)[1] for fires that occurred within Arizona during calendar years 2006 through 2010.[2] We obtained data for the Forest Service through its Fire Statistics System, extracting data from this system for all fires that occurred within the Coronado National Forest. We obtained data for the Department of the Interior's Bureau of Indian Affairs (BIA), Bureau of Land Management (BLM), and National Park Service (NPS) through its Wildland Fire Management Information Database, extracting data for all fires that occurred on Interior land units in Arizona. We obtained data for the Department of the Interior's Fish and Wildlife Service (FWS) through its Fire Management Information System, extracting data for all fires on the agency's land units within the Arizona border region. Lastly, we obtained data for lands managed by the state of Arizona, local governments, and private residents through the Fire and Aviation Management Data Warehouse, extracting data for all fires in the state of Arizona. From these data, we geographically located each fire based on latitude and longitude coordinates using geographic mapping software. We filtered the data to

---

[1]NIFC, located in Boise, Idaho, is the nation's logistical support center for controlling and extinguishing wildland fires and coordinates the mobilization of fire suppression supplies, equipment, and personnel at the federal, regional, and local levels. Additionally, NIFC maintains historical fire occurrence data for the Department of Agriculture's Forest Service and the Department of the Interior's Bureau of Indian Affairs, Bureau of Land Management, Fish and Wildlife Service, and National Park Service. NIFC also maintains historical fire occurrence data collected by state agencies, including the Arizona State Forestry Division, for fires on nonfederal lands.

[2]We did not include fires that occurred in calendar year 2011 because federal agencies do not collect fire documentation from local units or conduct quality assurance checks on data until the end of the calendar year, and, therefore, 2011 data are not yet complete and may not be reliable.

include only fires that occurred in Arizona within 100 miles of the U.S.-Mexico border. A number of records in the data set did not include geographic coordinates, preventing us from verifying the location of the fires—and, as a result, these fires are not included in our analysis. For the fires we were able to verify as within the Arizona border region, we then analyzed the data to identify the acreage burned and general cause—human or natural—cited for ignition. We assessed the reliability of the data we used by reviewing information about the underlying database systems and discussing the data with agency officials responsible for managing these databases, and determined that the data were sufficiently reliable for the purposes of presenting acreage burned and general cause of fires occurring during calendar years 2006 through 2010. Because NIFC does not manage the Department of Defense's (DOD) fire occurrence data, we also obtained information from DOD regarding wildland fire occurrence on its lands in the region and included these data in our overall figures. DOD officials identified and provided data for those fires on DOD-managed lands located within the Arizona border region. In our assessment of the data, we determined that these data were not sufficiently reliable for our purposes of presenting a comprehensive account of fires and acreage burned on DOD lands during calendar years 2006 through 2010. However, we included the information we were provided because they were the only data available.

During the course of our review, in 2011, two significant fires occurred in the Arizona border region—the Horseshoe Two and Monument fires. We could not include information on these two fires in our data analysis because at the time of our review, the data from the federal agencies on these fires were not complete and could not be determined as reliable. However, given the significance of these fires, we have included some descriptive and preliminary information about them throughout the report, as appropriate.

To determine the economic and environmental effects of significant human-caused wildland fires, we first identified those human-caused fires that burned 10 or more acres (which we consider significant fires for the purposes of this report) using the data collected in the previous objective. We then obtained additional information on these fires from the federal and state land management agencies included in our review. Each agency provided us with the amount of funds obligated to suppress the fires. Because some funding obligations for individual fires occurred over multiple years, we did not adjust these figures for inflation. In addition, the federal land management agencies provided us with data on environmental assessments conducted in response to these fires, as well as data on environmental restoration funds requested or provided in response to significant human-caused wildland fires. (The state of Arizona does not conduct such assessments or provide such funds.) We also identified the grazing allotments on Forest Service lands that were within the Arizona border region and could have been affected by human-caused wildland fires. For these allotments, we requested data from Forest Service's range management officials for any damages and repairs to these lands as a result of significant human-caused wildland fires. In addition, we reviewed studies conducted by academicians and wildland fire organizations on the economic impact of wildland fires.[3] Our review of the economic impact studies was not comprehensive to include all studies that may exist. Finally, we visited the region and discussed with federal, tribal, and state officials, as well as private industry representatives and private citizens in the ranching community, the economic and environmental damage that has occurred as a result of human-caused wildland fires.

To determine the extent to which federal agencies determined that illegal border crossers were the ignition source of wildland fires on federal lands, we reviewed agency documents to identify criteria for conducting investigations into the ignition source of human-caused wildland fires. We then identified all human-caused wildland fires and requested fire investigation reports for each fire from Forest Service and the Interior agencies. Because of extensive resource commitments on the part of the agencies in response to the severe 2011 wildland fire season in Arizona and the amount of resources needed to provide us with investigation reports, we limited our request to investigation reports for human-caused wildland fires burning at least 1 acre, which cumulatively comprised more than 99 percent of the acreage burned by human-caused wildland fires in the region from 2006 through 2010. We reviewed and evaluated the fire investigation reports to determine the extent to which fire investigations were conducted for human-caused wildland fires, and, for those fires for which investigations were conducted, we identified the extent to which officials identified illegal border crossers as the source of ignition. Additionally, we reviewed fire incident reports created by fire response

---

[3]Western Forestry Leadership Coalition, *The True Cost of Wildfire in the Western U.S.* (April 2010). Dennis L. Lynch, *Journal of Forestry*, "What Do Forest Fires Really Cost?" (September 2004). Bob Zybach, Michael Dubrasich, Greg Brenner, John Marker; Wildland Fire Lessons Learned Center; *U.S. Wildfire Cost-Plus-Loss Economics Project: The "One Pager" Checklist* (fall 2009).

personnel for all human-caused wildland fires to identify the extent to which they cited illegal border crossers as a potential source of ignition.

To determine ways in which the presence of illegal border crossers have affected fire response activities in the Arizona border region, we reviewed national and regional land management wildland fire guidance to identify any practices unique to regional land management units developed in response to illegal cross-border activity. We also identified and reviewed training materials and other documentation, such as the Forest Service's *Working Along the United States-Mexico Border* DVD and the Coronado National Forest's *Border Fire Response Protocol*, and interviewed land management, firefighting, and law enforcement officials to further identify specific actions taken in the border region. Further, during our site visits, we discussed with federal and nonfederal officials their experiences fighting wildland fires in the region.

We conducted this performance audit from December 2010 to November 2011 in accordance with generally accepted government auditing standards. Those standards require that we plan and perform the audit to obtain sufficient, appropriate evidence to provide a reasonable basis for our findings and conclusions based on our audit objectives. We believe that the evidence obtained provides a reasonable basis for our findings and conclusions based on our audit objectives.

Appendix II: Information on Significant Human-Caused Wildland Fires in the Arizona Border Region, 2006 through 2010

Table 3 shows size, duration, and suppression cost data for all significant human-caused wildland fires in the Arizona border region from 2006 through 2010.

Table 3: Acres Burned, Duration, and Suppression Costs for Significant Human-Caused Wildland Fires in the Arizona Border Region, 2006 through 2010

Year	Fire name	Land management agency	Acres burned	Duration (in days)	Suppression costs
2006	103	Forest Service	1,634	25	$2,506,792
2006	4E Levy	State of Arizona	63	2	33,516
2006	Antone	BIA	15	8	145
2006	Big Horn	State of Arizona	30	1	691
2006	Birch	State of Arizona	12	1	1,918
2006	Black Mesa	Forest Service	171	21	237,268
2006	Burro	Forest Service	370	27	1,358,207
2006	CA Runner	BIA	576	5	22,060
2006	Chimney	Forest Service	110	17	89,843
2006	Chuckles	State of Arizona	48	1	1,420
2006	Cienegas	State of Arizona	197	1	18,716
2006	City	FWS	21	2	262
2006	Clark	Forest Service	10	18	17,877
2006	Confluence	BLM	37	3	16,008
2006	Curly Horse	BLM	1,565	2	20,148
2006	Early Morning	State of Arizona	50	2	34,947
2006	Eldon	State of Arizona	10	1	2,068
2006	Eloy	State of Arizona	20	1	803
2006	Fatman	BIA	10	8	6,899
2006	Fellows	BLM	22	1	726
2006	Friendly	State of Arizona	30	1	493
2006	Gu jas 1	FWS	10	1	3,986
2006	Harque	State of Arizona	80	1	6,402
2006	Hidden	BLM	20	1	318
2006	Hope	FWS	431	5	71,656
2006	I-10 MM75	State of Arizona	18	1	1,412
2006	ID	State of Arizona	20	1	353
2006	Levy	State of Arizona	150	2	12,672
2006	Lime	State of Arizona	12	1	1,869
2006	Lobo	Forest Service	26	31	78,485
2006	Marshall	BLM	14	5	13,807

Year	Fire name	Land management agency	Acres burned	Duration (in days)	Suppression costs
2006	McNeal	State of Arizona	11	1	2,853
2006	Mesa	BIA	26	11	2,871
2006	Migrant	FWS	30	1	10,972
2006	Milligan	State of Arizona	15	1	822
2006	MM 4	BIA	15	7	12,149
2006	Monitor	DOD	10	a	b
2006	Montezuma 1	Forest Service	4,191	8	284,294
2006	Mustang	State of Arizona	10	1	2,301
2006	NA	DOD	20	1	b
2006	Oatman	BLM	593	2	27,464
2006	Painted	State of Arizona	200	1	5,463
2006	Pit Field	State of Arizona	60	a	565
2006	Playa	State of Arizona	26	1	9,856
2006	Rainbow Ranch	State of Arizona	60	1	1,145
2006	Ralston	State of Arizona	20	1	272
2006	Run Away	BLM	113	2	63,124
2006	Saddle	BLM	1,200	3	88,158
2006	Shadow	BLM	41	5	14,617
2006	Sixty Niner	State of Arizona	227	0	4,029
2006	Sunizona	State of Arizona	10	1	893
2006	Tacna Mohawk	BLM	143	3	6,259
2006	Theba II	BLM	38	2	30,690
2006	Thornton	State of Arizona	25	1	211
2006	Tower 62	DOD	10 to 20	a	b
2006	Tweedy	State of Arizona	50	1	204
2006	West	BIA	26	10	1,273
2006	Williamson Valley FD	State of Arizona	40	a	160
2006	Windy	BLM	128	9	7,246
2006	Yellow South	State of Arizona	10	a	1,293
2007	Altar	State of Arizona	30	1	2,666
2007	Austin	State of Arizona	240	1	1,526
2007	Brainard # 2	DOD	27	a	b
2007	Buckeye	BLM	68	7	221,815
2007	Buena	FWS	1,151	4	132,409
2007	Christmas	DOD	500	a	b
2007	Chui-Chu # 2	BIA	40	1	1,252
2007	Cobre 2	Forest Service	160	9	159,179

Year	Fire name	Land management agency	Acres burned	Duration (in days)	Suppression costs
2007	Copper	Forest Service	87	7	76,475
2007	Cottonwood	BLM	14	44	95,162
2007	County 9	BLM	17	7	20,790
2007	County 9th	State of Arizona	10	2	33,800
2007	Cowlic	BIA	37	3	15,005
2007	Easter Fire	BIA	100	2	0
2007	Elgin	State of Arizona	600	1	19,799
2007	Fields	State of Arizona	15	1	681
2007	Fresno	Forest Service	321	16	0
2007	Highway 92 Complex	Forest Service	46	7	76,104
2007	Honnus	FWS	162	2	14,498
2007	HWY 92	DOD	30	a	b
2007	Kino	Forest Service	100	5	13,669
2007	Kitt Peak	BIA	12	2	11,747
2007	Lucky 3	State of Arizona	100	1	41,452
2007	Marble	State of Arizona	75	1	1,570
2007	Maverick	DOD	475	a	b
2007	Norton	BLM	66	4	94,976
2007	Orange	State of Arizona	50	3	26,139
2007	Parks	Forest Service	120	8	21,751
2007	Parks Two	Forest Service	30	8	0
2007	Power Line	State of Arizona	30	1	0
2007	Railroad 2	State of Arizona	225	2	9,029
2007	Range 8	DOD	46	a	b
2007	Range 9 #2	DOD	300	a	b
2007	Route 20	BIA	109	1	0
2007	RP	Forest Service	12	11	438
2007	San Antonio	Forest Service	1,543	12	264,989
2007	San Luis	BLM	69	53	19,241
2007	San Rafael	State of Arizona	753	3	37,460
2007	Santa Margarita	FWS	41	3	3,352
2007	Sasco	State of Arizona	40	1	1,061
2007	Stronghold	State of Arizona	10	a	3,346
2007	Sulphur	Forest Service	10	9	2,993
2007	Sunland	State of Arizona	18	2	758
2007	Sutherland	Forest Service	27	7	3,576
2007	Walnut Gap	State of Arizona	10	1	3,176

Year	Fire name	Land management agency	Acres burned	Duration (in days)	Suppression costs
2007	Yaqui	Forest Service	161	9	186,179
2008	103	Forest Service	378	7	28,038
2008	104	Forest Service	350	8	41,594
2008	7th AVE	BIA	30	7	52,542
2008	Alamo	Forest Service	5,070	20	1,730,669
2008	Apache	Forest Service	10	5	c
2008	Area West	Forest Service	125	7	7,967
2008	Back Pack	State of Arizona	20	2	13,829
2008	Backyard	State of Arizona	19	a	471
2008	B-Box	State of Arizona	24	1	7,345
2008	Bear 2	Forest Service	280	8	4,669
2008	Beehive	Forest Service	325	22	1,114,018
2008	Bell	State of Arizona	40	1	1,556
2008	Buck	Forest Service	2,021	9	181,893
2008	Cantina	Forest Service	35	6	30,902
2008	Castle Rock	Forest Service	40	4	9,720
2008	Cemetery	BIA	160	1	0
2008	Coronado	NPS	80	3	105,516
2008	Cowlic	BIA	15	1	0
2008	Dome	BLM	220	24	195,560
2008	Drain Fire	BIA	33	7	2,519
2008	Early Morning	State of Arizona	20	1	987
2008	Encinas Tank	Forest Service	25	8	28,436
2008	Escapule Trail	BLM	12	2	5,179
2008	Fisher	BLM	69	1	5,080
2008	Frye Mesa	Forest Service	3,094	17	1,469,967
2008	High Gates	FWS	90	1	12,812
2008	High Lonesome	Forest Service	317	9	16,518
2008	Kansas Settlement	State of Arizona	750	2	17,192
2008	Levee Road	BLM	57	6	107,943
2008	Lochiel	State of Arizona	88	1	8,416
2008	Lonesome	State of Arizona	125	a	38,943
2008	Meadow	Forest Service	3,876	17	41,402
2008	Milepost 6	Forest Service	13	7	30,340
2008	Mission	NPS	110	6	79,472
2008	Mohawk	BLM	69	19	64,638
2008	Moon Canyon	BLM	750	4	245,692

Year	Fire name	Land management agency	Acres burned	Duration (in days)	Suppression costs
2008	Omega	FWS	27	2	2,557
2008	Pomerene	State of Arizona	20	1	5,904
2008	Pozo	FWS	65	3	14,630
2008	Pozo 2	FWS	53	3	0
2008	Pozo 3	FWS	66	3	0
2008	Pozo 4	FWS	75	3	0
2008	San Antonio	Forest Service	24	5	3,407
2008	Silva	BIA	22	6	19,928
2008	Solano	BIA	2,575	12	1,777,243
2008	Sunny	State of Arizona	10	1	1,037
2008	Tomb	State of Arizona	378	2	8,941
2008	Trigo	FWS	35	17	29,891
2008	Tubac	State of Arizona	15	4	4,928
2008	Valentine	BLM	99	8	43,592
2008	Ventana	Forest Service	20	11	48,842
2008	Warsaw	Forest Service	15	14	29,941
2008	Whitewater	State of Arizona	15	1	4,743
2008	York	State of Arizona	30	1	2,384
2009	103	Forest Service	314	9	13,236
2009	222	Forest Service	105	4	57,226
2009	A-Bar	Forest Service	16	14	90,340
2009	Apache	NPS	54	2	1,378
2009	ATV	BIA	398	10	155,987
2009	Aztec	BLM	470	7	340,506
2009	Bear	Forest Service	15	5	324,893
2009	Bright	BLM	75	3	19,065
2009	Buckeye	BLM	289	4	354,010
2009	Canelo	Forest Service	4,208	16	1,847,475
2009	Canoa	State of Arizona	70	2	2,130
2009	Cisco	State of Arizona	160	[a]	10,342
2009	Dee Road	State of Arizona	17	1	1,450
2009	Diamondback	State of Arizona	48	3	44,367
2009	Dome Valley	State of Arizona	84	3	52,002
2009	Dry Canyon	Forest Service	17	4	2,575
2009	Eagle Lake	Forest Service	105	[a]	56,229
2009	Ehrenberg	BLM	60	3	109,438
2009	Elgin	BLM	379	4	288,694

Year	Fire name	Land management agency	Acres burned	Duration (in days)	Suppression costs
2009	Elk Horn	BLM	23,668	11	443,517
2009	FA Bell Ranch Road	State of Arizona	60	a	0
2009	Ferosa	Forest Service	12	4	23,320
2009	Fish	Forest Service	1,050	12	157,687
2009	Fort Bowie	State of Arizona	16	1	2,717
2009	Fresnal Fire	BIA	247	6	419,453
2009	Gate 7	Forest Service	15	18	63,792
2009	Gleeson	State of Arizona	782	3	144,244
2009	Gleeson Road	State of Arizona	23	2	1,646
2009	Gu jas	FWS	12	2	1,197
2009	Hay Flat	State of Arizona	35	1	5,516
2009	Hog	Forest Service	16,802	21	725,994
2009	Irwin	Forest Service	22	2	2,517
2009	Island	FWS	102	11	293,274
2009	Kudu	BIA	76	5	33,521
2009	Lesna Peak	Forest Service	756	14	47,142
2009	Little Alamo	Forest Service	851	8	69,940
2009	Lochiel	Forest Service	2,660	14	404,504
2009	Montana	Forest Service	2,455	38	333,691
2009	Muchacho	BIA	23	4	41,847
2009	Mule Pass	BLM	122	4	716,162
2009	Museum	State of Arizona	29	4	45,599
2009	Nugget	Forest Service	42	22	228,602
2009	O'Leary	State of Arizona	11	1	0
2009	Pete's Kitchen	State of Arizona	152	2	30,876
2009	Pothole	Forest Service	25	10	26,266
2009	Power	BLM	260	9	122,980
2009	Quail	State of Arizona	37	3	48,870
2009	Rest Area Fire	BIA	386	3	256
2009	Robbins Butte	BLM	32	5	50,683
2009	Route 35	BIA	27	2	4,443
2009	Ruby	Forest Service	130	a	116,386
2009	San Jose de Sonoita	State of Arizona	19	1	3,144
2009	San Juan	BIA	9,200	8	178,157
2009	School 2	Forest Service	24	4	5,032
2009	School Canyon	Forest Service	50	21	13,096
2009	Three Peaks	BLM	5,735	12	207,841

Year	Fire name	Land management agency	Acres burned	Duration (in days)	Suppression costs
2009	Trestle	BLM	16	2	13,344
2009	Turkey	State of Arizona	129	3	20,243
2009	Turtleback	BLM	160	36	36,241
2009	Van Ness	State of Arizona	36	1	15,932
2009	Washington	Forest Service	84	6	72,955
2009	Whitewater	State of Arizona	23	1	8,825
2009	Willow	BLM	10	8	28,442
2009	Yellow Jacket	Forest Service	27	8	12,244
2010	133	BIA	57	2	9,338
2010	99 Bar	FWS	18	4	27,382
2010	Chino	Forest Service	21	5	19,345
2010	Fisher Hill	State of Arizona	52	2	1,164
2010	Five	Forest Service	73	6	14,734
2010	Fort Fire	Forest Service	50	11	193,779
2010	Fraguita	Forest Service	1,914	10	260,980
2010	Horseshoe	Forest Service	3,401	55	10,185,914
2010	Hunter	Forest Service	33	20	206,145
2010	Indian School	BIA	17	17	16,401
2010	Jarillas	Forest Service	20	8	39,031
2010	Kudu Ranch	BIA	10	4	41,754
2010	Lone Mountain	Forest Service	486	10	61,442
2010	New Year	Forest Service	38	15	17,859
2010	Southfork	Forest Service	103	28	531,173
2010	Talley	BIA	136	22	27,006
2010	Yellow Jacket	Forest Service	25	12	$86,515

Source: GAO analysis of Forest Service, Interior, Arizona Forestry Division, and DOD data.

Notes: Duration was identified by determining the days elapsed between when a fire was reported "discovered" and when it was declared either "controlled" or "out," depending on what information agencies report in their fire occurrence data.

[a]Data provided by federal and state agencies did not include enough information for us to determine duration.

[b]The Department of Defense did not provide us with information on suppression costs associated with each fire.

[c]The Forest Service did not provide us with information on suppression costs associated with the 2008 Apache Fire.

Appendix III: Additional Information on Wildland Fires That Federal Agencies Suspect Were Ignited by Illegal Border Crossers

Table 4 provides information on those wildland fires in which officials documented through formal fire investigations that illegal border crossers are a suspected cause for the wildland fire.

Table 4: Wildland Fires That Burned One or More Acres for Which Formal Fire Investigations Identified Illegal Border Crossers as a Suspected Cause

Year	Fire name	Land management agency
2006	Black Mesa	Forest Service
2006	Chimney	Forest Service
2006	Christen	Forest Service
2007	Bates Well	NPS
2007	Cobre 2	Forest Service
2007	Javelina	Forest Service
2007	Parks	Forest Service
2007	Santa Margarita	FWS
2008	High Gates	FWS
2008	Omega	FWS
2008	Pesquiera	Forest Service
2008	Pozo	FWS
2008	Pozo 2	FWS
2008	Pozo 3	FWS
2008	Pozo 4	FWS
2008	Warsaw	Forest Service
2009	A-Bar	Forest Service
2009	Bear	Forest Service
2009	Canelo	Forest Service
2009	Ferosa	Forest Service
2009	Hog	Forest Service
2009	Potrero	Forest Service
2009	School Canyon	Forest Service
2009	School 2	Forest Service
2009	Washington	Forest Service
2010	Fort Fire	Forest Service
2010	Horseshoe	Forest Service
2010	Lone Mountain	Forest Service
2010	Southfork	Forest Service
2010	Yellow Jacket	Forest Service

Source: GAO analysis of Forest Service and Interior data.

In addition to the formal investigations into ignition sources, fire incident reports—documentation completed by fire responders on the size, location, and general cause of each fire—sometimes contain fire responders' views on the cause of the wildland fire. Fire incident reports we reviewed noted illegal border crossers as a suspected cause for 57 wildland fires in the region. However, the purpose of these reports is to document general wildland fire occurrence data and the reports are not indicative of a formal investigation into the fire's origin (see fig. 5 for location of wildland fires). Table 5 provides information on wildland fires in which officials documented through fire incident reports that illegal border crossers are a suspected cause for the wildland fire.

Table 5: Wildland Fires for Which Fire Incident Reports Indicate Illegal Border Crossers as a Suspected Cause

Year	Fire name	Land management agency
2006	103	Forest Service
2006	B.P. camp fire	BIA
2006	Backpack	BIA
2006	Cerrito	BLM
2006	Creek Bed 62	NPS
2006	E. Monument	NPS
2006	Guijas 1	FWS
2006	K-5	BIA
2006	MP75.1	BIA
2006	Pisinemo	BIA
2006	SR Ranch	BIA
2006	Twig Fire	BIA
2007	86 Fire	BIA
2007	Bates Well	NPS
2007	Bates Well #2	NPS
2007	Bates Well #3	NPS
2007	Buena	FWS
2007	Sutherland	Forest Service
2007	UDA	BIA
2008	Alfonzo	BIA
2008	Barry Goldwater	BLM
2008	Bear Canyon	Forest Service
2008	BP	BLM
2008	Cowlic	BIA

Year	Fire name	Land management agency
2008	Dirty Wash Fire	NPS
2008	Fence	BIA
2008	First Time	BIA
2008	Mission	NPS
2008	PW	BIA
2008	Wattle	NPS
2009	Artesia Fire	BIA
2009	Bates Well	BLM
2009	Bay Fire	BIA
2009	Border Patrol 2	BIA
2009	Camp Fire	BIA
2009	Cocopah	BIA
2009	Coldfields	BIA
2009	Como Fire	BIA
2009	Dripping Springs	NPS
2009	First 90	NPS
2009	Iron Stand	BIA
2009	Mike Fire	BIA
2009	Milepost 137.5	BIA
2009	Nolic	BIA
2009	Post #7	BIA
2009	Route 35	BIA
2009	San Juan	BIA
2009	Vamori Fire	BIA
2010	Armenta	NPS
2010	Cinco	NPS
2010	Four Arm Cactus	NPS
2010	Fort Apache Fire	BIA
2010	Joes	NPS
2010	Nolic Fire	BIA
2010	Platt	BLM
2010	Ranch	BIA
2010	Signal	BIA

Source: GAO analysis of Forest Service and Interior data.

Note: According to data provided by DOD, officials identified illegal border crossers as a suspected cause of 16 wildland fires on DOD-managed lands. However, this information was not obtained through a formal investigation and it was not documented in a fire incident report.

Figure 5: Locations of Wildland Fires for Which Agency Fire Incident Reports Identified Illegal Border Crossers as a Suspected Ignition Source

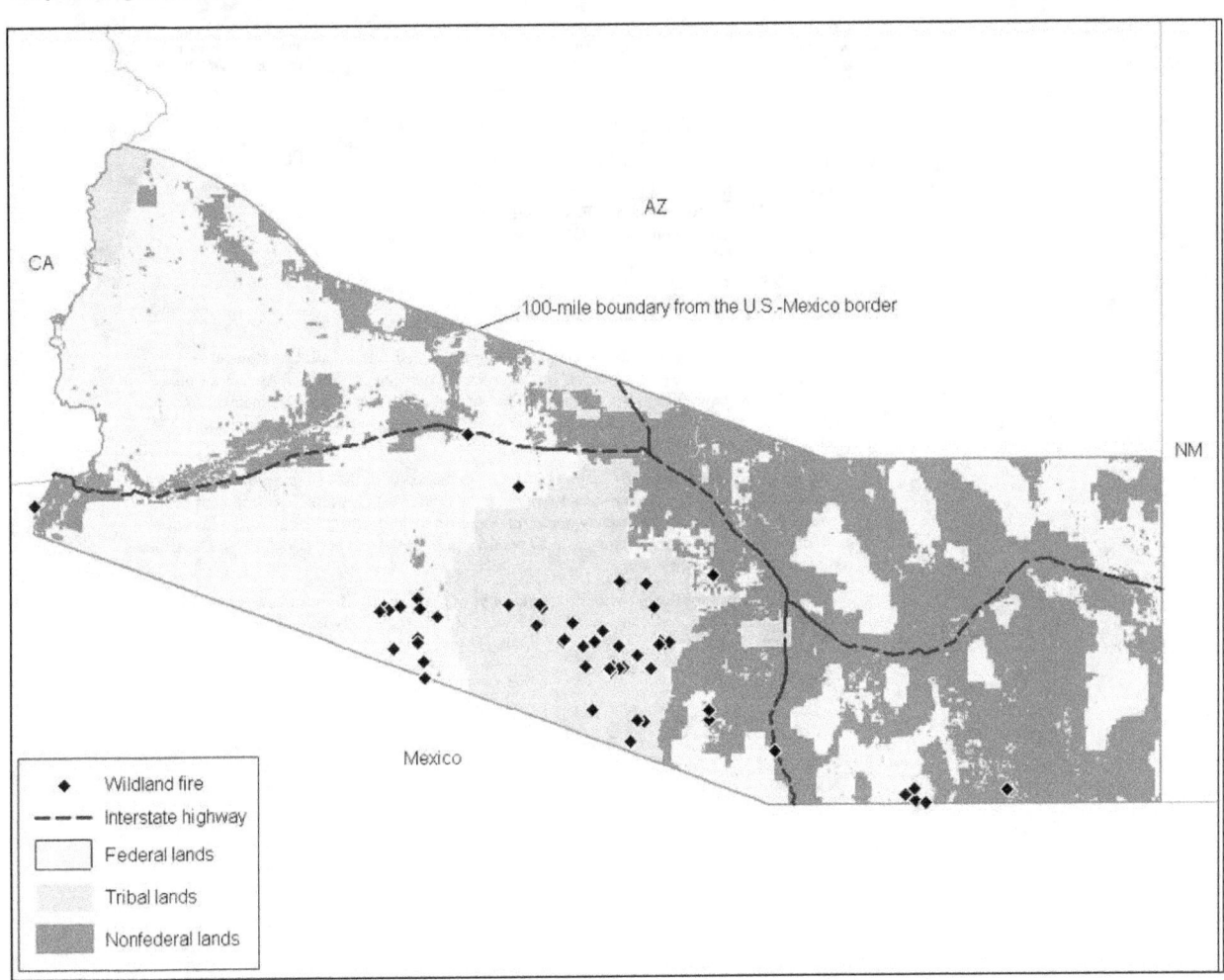

Source: GAO analysis of Forest Service and Interior data; MapInfo (map).

Appendix IV: Comments from the U.S. Department of Agriculture

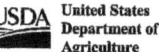

| USDA | United States Department of Agriculture | Forest Service | Washington Office | 1400 Independence Avenue, SW Washington, DC 20250 |

File Code: 1420

Date: OCT 2 0 2011

Ms. Anu K. Mittal
Director, Natural Resources and Environment
U.S. Government Accountability Office
441 G Street, NW
Washington, DC 20548

Dear Ms. Mittal:

Thank you for the opportunity to review and comment on the draft U.S. Government Accountability Office (GAO) Report on "Arizona Border Region: Federal Agencies Could Better Utilize Law Enforcement Resources in Support of Wildland Fire Management Activities" (GAO-12-73). The Forest Service has reviewed the report and concurs with the report's observations and recommendations.

The agency does not have any major comments on the report or the recommendations, except to mention with regard to Recommendation 3 that the Southwest Coordinating Group has been working on a standard interagency border protocol (to include most if not all of the Coronado National Forest guidance). This protocol would guide firefighters and also apply to Department of the Interior agencies.

Thank you again for the opportunity to review your draft report. If you have any questions, please contact Donna M. Carmical, Chief Financial Officer, at 202-205-1321 or dcarmical@fs.fed.us.

Sincerely,

THOMAS L. TIDWELL
Chief

                    Caring for the Land and Serving People   Printed on Recycled Paper

Appendix V: Comments from the Department of Homeland Security

U.S. Department of Homeland Security
Washington, DC 20528

Homeland Security

October 25, 2011

Anu K. Mittal
Director, National Resources and Environment
441 G Street, NW
U.S. Government Accountability Office
Washington, DC 20548

Re: Draft Report GAO-12-73, "ARIZONA BORDER REGION: Federal Agencies Could
     Better Utilize Law Enforcement Resources in Support of Wildland Fire Management
     Activities"

Dear Ms. Mittal:

Thank you for the opportunity to comment on this draft report. The U.S. Department of
Homeland Security (DHS) appreciates the U.S. Government and Accountability Office's
(GAO) work in planning and conducting its review and issuing this report.

The Department is pleased to note GAO's acknowledgment of the complex and diverse
challenges that federal land management agencies in the Arizona border region face in
carrying out their responsibilities, including those posed by illegal border crossers. We note
the report does not contain any recommendations specifically directed at the DHS. The
Department, particularly U.S. Customs and Border Protection, however, remains committed
to continuing its work with interagency partners, such as the U.S. Departments of Agriculture
and Interior, to identify and mitigate adverse impacts to wildland fire management activities.

Again, thank you for the opportunity to review and comment on this draft report. We look
forward to working with you on future Homeland Security issues.

Sincerely,

Jim H. Crumpacker
Director
Departmental GAO-OIG Liaison Office

Appendix VI: GAO Contact and Staff Acknowledgments

GAO Contact	Anu K. Mittal, (202) 512-3841 or mittala@gao.gov
Staff Acknowledgments	In addition to the contact named above, Steve Gaty, Assistant Director; Mehrzad Nadji; Alison O'Neill; Steven Putansu; Jeanette Soares; Jay Spaan; and Matt Tabbert made significant contributions to this report.

GAO's Mission	The Government Accountability Office, the audit, evaluation, and investigative arm of Congress, exists to support Congress in meeting its constitutional responsibilities and to help improve the performance and accountability of the federal government for the American people. GAO examines the use of public funds; evaluates federal programs and policies; and provides analyses, recommendations, and other assistance to help Congress make informed oversight, policy, and funding decisions. GAO's commitment to good government is reflected in its core values of accountability, integrity, and reliability.
Obtaining Copies of GAO Reports and Testimony	The fastest and easiest way to obtain copies of GAO documents at no cost is through GAO's website (www.gao.gov). Each weekday afternoon, GAO posts on its website newly released reports, testimony, and correspondence. To have GAO e-mail you a list of newly posted products, go to www.gao.gov and select "E-mail Updates."
Order by Phone	The price of each GAO publication reflects GAO's actual cost of production and distribution and depends on the number of pages in the publication and whether the publication is printed in color or black and white. Pricing and ordering information is posted on GAO's website, http://www.gao.gov/ordering.htm. Place orders by calling (202) 512-6000, toll free (866) 801-7077, or TDD (202) 512-2537. Orders may be paid for using American Express, Discover Card, MasterCard, Visa, check, or money order. Call for additional information.
Connect with GAO	Connect with GAO on Facebook, Flickr, Twitter, and YouTube. Subscribe to our RSS Feeds or E-mail Updates. Listen to our Podcasts. Visit GAO on the web at www.gao.gov.
To Report Fraud, Waste, and Abuse in Federal Programs	Contact: Website: www.gao.gov/fraudnet/fraudnet.htm E-mail: fraudnet@gao.gov Automated answering system: (800) 424-5454 or (202) 512-7470
Congressional Relations	Ralph Dawn, Managing Director, dawnr@gao.gov, (202) 512-4400 U.S. Government Accountability Office, 441 G Street NW, Room 7125 Washington, DC 20548
Public Affairs	Chuck Young, Managing Director, youngc1@gao.gov, (202) 512-4800 U.S. Government Accountability Office, 441 G Street NW, Room 7149 Washington, DC 20548